THE ECUMENICAL GRAIL PSALTER

SINGING VERSION

The Benedictine Monks
of Conception Abbey

GIA PUBLICATIONS, INC.
CHICAGO

The Ecumenical Grail Psalter, Singing Version

G-9088
ISBN: 978-1-62277-169-1

The Ecumenical Grail Psalter is *not approved for liturgical use in the Catholic Church*, which retains for its liturgical use the original *Revised Grail Psalms* as approved by both the USCCB and Congregation for Divine Worship and the Discipline of the Sacraments.

Printed in the United States of America.

Introduction to The Ecumenical Grail Psalter

The Songs of Israel—The Songs of the Church

In the late 1940s, Father Patrick Cummins, OSB, a monk of Conception Abbey and a scholar and translator of Scripture in his own right, wrote the following definition in the Introduction to his own unpublished translation of the Book of Psalms:

> What is a psalm? Is it a prayer? A rhythmic prayer? A hymn? An oriental hymn? A Semitic hymn? A Hebrew hymn? The answer to all these questions is an ascending Yes. Hence, if we look at human literature as an ascending pyramid, then that pyramid is crowned by the Psalter. [Human beings] are most godlike when [they] sing to God. And among those who sing to God the Hebrew psalmist stands highest. In universality of sentiment, in keenness of conception, in rhythm of speech, in beauty of imagery, the Hebrew singer has no rivals.

The Psalms have been the prayer book of both Jews and Christians from their beginnings as peoples of faith and worship. The Gospels make clear that Jesus himself used and prayed the Psalms during his earthly life, quoting from them more than from any other book of Scripture. The old adage *Lex orandi lex credendi*—which means "the way we pray is the way we believe"—suggests how significant these prayers have been in the formation of communities of believers. The Book of Psalms provides words that bring meaning to our search for God in all of life's circumstances: in fear or joy, struggle or hope, pain or praise, despair or thanksgiving. Though some of these texts have been used for more than two millennia, the prayers of the Psalter retain a freshness that enables them to speak with poignant clarity to each succeeding generation, drawing those who read them into the deepest purpose of human life: to abide in the presence of God.

How often in life do we find ourselves struggling to find words that express the manifold movements of the human heart! The Psalms provide access to that unique chamber of the heart where one stands most free and open before God. To our surprise, we find ourselves thinking, "These words express my inmost thoughts and feelings better than I could myself. They say what I want to say to God." The character of the Psalms is universal and classic, touching the human heart and giving voice to the most intimate motions of our souls before the One who is transcendent and immanent, incomprehensible yet alarmingly close. The Psalms take us from the heights of praise to the depths of distress with words that invariably foster a life-giving hope. They are inspired!

Rightly have the Psalms been called a school of prayer. These prayers give voice to many of the experiences presented in the stories of the Bible—they come to us as words that have already been cried, shouted, and sung throughout the centuries by people of faith. Human struggles with encompassing illness, imminent death, implacable enemies, and hostile powers find voice in the Psalms, which give expression to the fears and uncertainties that trouble the human condition. Similarly, the joy of victory, gratitude for prayers answered, and wonder at the marvels of creation all enter into the praise that is lifted up to God who brings life into being and rules the created world. The Psalms attest with unshakable conviction that the one and almighty God who touches every movement of history and each human life is the focus of all praise, the healer of all ills, and the source of all blessing.

The Psalms, then, are the prayer book of the Bible. They are appropriate responses to every situation encountered in the pages of sacred Scripture. In Christian congregations, having heard the word of God proclaimed in the readings, we respond with a psalm; its words echo those of the reading, lifting our hearts in prayer. As God has spoken to the assembly through the sacred word, so through the psalm do the people respond to God. Such dialogue is the heart of any relationship with God. The Psalms are an instrument of that dialogue when prayed by people of faith.

To the superlative status of the Psalms as literary expression, we may add the observation that the various genres or literary forms found in them express the wide-ranging life situations and the varying moods of the person of faith before God. The *hymn* lifts up praise to the God who has created the world and all its wonders. The *lament* brings before God the pain of alienation from God and neighbor, the struggle with doubts and fears, the anger that rises from disgrace and mistreatment, the fear of threatening illness and approaching death, the anguish of both individual loss and communal tribulation. The *thanksgiving* reminds the community that gratitude is owed to God who hears and answers those in need. The *wisdom* psalms reflect the insight and spiritual understanding that fosters a life of faith, hope, and love.

Many of the Psalms open with unfamiliar expressions like "A *mitzmor* of David, with instrumental music, on the *gittith*." The names of Korah (Psalms 42, 44–49) and Asaph (Psalm 50, 73–83), often attached to such expressions, identify two of the musical guilds of the Jerusalem temple, where the Psalms were originally prayed. Many of these phrases indicate that the Psalms were meant to be sung, often with specified musical accompaniment. The Hebrew title for the Book of Psalms is *Sepher Tehillim*, or "a Book of Sung Praises," further indicating how these prayers were expected to be rendered. Any text is clothed and elevated by music; melody holds a special power to express what may not be possible for spoken words alone. It gives added expression that not only enhances the meaning but also raises the words to the level of inspiring prayer. This truth provides yet another insight into the profound message of the Psalms. They were created to be sung, which gives the words a second soul.

As songs of the early Church, the Psalms were not merely prayer, however; they were prophecy as well. In Luke's account of the risen Christ appearing and speaking to his disciples in Jerusalem, Jesus affirms: "'These are my words that I spoke to you while I was still with you, that everything written about me in the law of Moses and in the prophets and psalms must be fulfilled.' Then he opened their minds to understand the scriptures" (Luke 24:44 NRSV). The authors of the New Testament use the Psalms extensively to speak of the mystery of Jesus Christ as Messiah, the Anointed One.[1] The Psalms hold a key to understanding Jesus as the long-awaited Messiah. And as the early Church began to develop its yearly round of celebrating the life, suffering, death, and resurrection of Christ, the *messianic* psalms played a substantial role in unfolding that great mystery of faith.

In Praise of the 1963 Grail Psalms

The Grail Psalms (1963) provided one of the most successful of the vernacular texts to emerge from the liturgical reforms of the 1960s. These texts had originally been translated into English from the Psalms of the French *Bible de Jérusalem*; they proved remarkably sensitive to the requirements of choral recitation and chant, were adaptable to the requirements of varied musical settings, and were expressed in a literary style that was easily accessible to ordinary readers. The 1963 Grail Psalms became a primary vehicle for Christian prayer; over the years since, they have come to shape the worship and spiritual life of countless communities and individuals in the English-speaking world. They opened the door by which many people could become familiar with the language and imagery of the Bible in ways that were inviting, enriching, and satisfying.

What are the qualities that distinguish the 1963 Grail Psalms? For many, the Grail Psalms became an avenue into understanding and appreciating the whole of the Old Testament. Hearing this account of how God was for the chosen people both victorious warrior and gentle shepherd,

---

[1] Several salient passages in which the New Testament authors quote the Psalms are: Mt 21:9//Mk11:9//Lk 19:38//Jn 12:13 quotes Ps 118:26; Mt 21:42//Mk 12:10–11//Lk 20:17 quotes Ps 118:22–23; Mt 22:44//Mk 12:36//Lk 20:42–43 quotes Ps 110:1; Mt 27:46 quotes Ps 22:2; Jn 19:24 quotes Ps 22:19; Jn 19:36 quotes Ps 34:19; Acts 2:34–35 quotes Ps 110:1; Acts 4:25–26 quotes Ps 2:1–2; Heb 1:5 quotes Ps 2:7; Heb 1:6 quotes Ps 97:7; Heb 1:7 quotes Ps 104:4 (LXX); Heb 1:8 quotes Ps 45:7–8; Heb 1:10–12 quotes Ps 102:26–28; Heb 1:13 quotes Ps 110:1; Heb 2:6–7 quotes Ps 8: 5–7.

the One who hears our single voice in prayer and who calls us to live faithfully—this made clear how intimate was the relationship each person shares with God. Simple expressions continue to resonate in the hearts of many who pray these texts, bespeaking their own prayer to God: "Be still and know that I am God" (Ps 46:11), "Create a pure heart in me, O God" (Ps 51:12), "Mercy and faithfulness have met, justice and peace have embraced" (Ps 85:11), "Friend and neighbor you have taken away; my one companion is darkness" (Ps 88:19), and "O LORD, you search me and you know me; you know my resting and my rising" (Ps 139:1–2a). Such phrases lend themselves to effortless recall, becoming the very fabric of the interior life.

The "sprung rhythm" in which the Grail Psalms were composed made them easy to recite in common (that is, in a group setting) and easy to sing as chant.[2] Setting aside the stricter expectations of more formal poetic conventions, this rhythmic style imitates regular speech patterns more closely. Sprung rhythm possesses in vocal use something both natural and beautiful, a quality of simplicity and regularity one finds in reading through the lines of a Grail Psalm. The very ebb and flow of the lines make these psalms conducive to prayer and reflection. And importantly, these rhythmic patterns bear a notable similarity to those in which the Hebrew psalms were composed and are still evident today when they are prayed aloud in the synagogue.

The language of the 1963 Grail Psalms was straightforward and accessible; the person in the pew did not need a background in scriptural theology to grasp the general import of the text. At the same time, its poetic quality and beauty also could inspire the sensitive reader to ponder on further levels these simple yet profound and noble expressions of faith. It gave those who prayed it a language steeped in the inspired word, language for petition, praise, thanksgiving, confidence, hope, courage, faith, sorrow,

---

[2] Sprung rhythm imitates natural speech patterns, designating a certain number of major accents per line, while having an unfixed number of unstressed syllables, with no more than four syllables between each foot. Gerard Manley Hopkins, the nineteenth-century British poet and Jesuit, coined the expression, calling it "the most natural of things" in spoken poetry.

human struggle before God, and love of God, neighbor, and creation. It gave people a form for their own internal conversation with God.

Why a Revision of the 1963 Grail Psalms?

The excellent qualities of the 1963 Grail Psalms might give rise to the question, Why make a revision? There are several compelling reasons. As with anything that has generated such positive appreciation, there are also negative criticisms to be made. While the rhythmic quality and consistency in the Grail Psalms merits praise, the sometimes strict adherence to these rhythmic patterns too frequently forced its translators to *paraphrase* the text rather than translate it literally. Our revision maintains the sprung rhythm while at the same time striving for a more authentic translation of many paraphrased lines. Those who have prayed the 1963 Grail Psalms for many years will find great similarities in this revision, but will also encounter some very different expressions of language in the newly translated elements.

Furthermore, considerable strides have been made in biblical scholarship since the 1950s and early 1960s, when the Grail translations were produced. We have come to a better understanding of many of the rhetorical devices used by the Hebrew psalmists, and these insights have been incorporated into the revision. Our understanding of the literary genres and patterns of thought found in the Psalms has also developed greatly; this too enables us to translate these ancient texts with greater accuracy.

And while building on the good and inspiring elements of the first edition has the potential to provide continuity for those who have prayed the Grail Psalms during these past five decades, we must be cognizant of those who will use this Psalter in the future. It is our genuine hope that this revision of the Grail Psalms will be an effective vehicle for prayer, contemplation, and interior renewal of heart. Even as it seeks to present more authentic renderings of the ancient texts, it also hopes to provide more inclusive forms of expression—forms that are often truer to the original Hebrew than were the 1963 Grail Psalms. If this revision of the 1963 Grail Psalms helps to forward the renewal that every heart constantly seeks, it will have fulfilled its purpose.

We have retained in this edition the practice of indicating the accents of the sprung rhythm for recitation and chanting of the Psalms. It is our hope that these marked accents will facilitate a prayerful and inspiring chanting or reading of the Psalms for communities who pray the Liturgy of the Hours in common, or for individuals who might wish to recite or chant them aloud.

Why an Ecumenical Edition of *The Revised Grail Psalms*?

On 19 March 2010, the Congregation for Divine Worship and the Discipline of the Sacraments granted a *recognitio* (that is, permission for a text to be used in the Roman Catholic liturgy) to *The Revised Grail Psalms*. As noted above, this edition was prepared as a *liturgical translation*, intended for use in the Roman Catholic liturgy. Guiding principles for translation were provided by *Liturgiam Authenticam*, a document of the Congregation for Divine Worship and the Discipline of the Sacraments, and the process took into account the historical use of the Book of Psalms in the Church's liturgy. Thus while the translation is primarily based on the Hebrew text of the Psalms from the *Biblica Hebraica Stuttgartensia*, it is important to recognize that because of their influence on the Church's use of the Psalter, the texts of the Greek Septuagint and the Latin *Vulgata* and *Nova Vulgata* were also taken into account for this translation specifically intended for use in the Roman Catholic liturgy.

Within a year of its publication, Christian leaders from groups beyond the Roman Catholic communion expressed appreciation for certain aspects of the texts of *The Revised Grail Psalms*, particularly the poetic quality of the text and the sprung rhythm, which facilitates recitation, chant, and musical settings of the texts. Among these leaders were an Episcopalian bishop, a bishop of the Evangelical Lutheran Church of America, the president of a Baptist seminary, and the academic dean of a Calvinist seminary. They further inquired if we might consider publishing another edition of *The Revised Grail Psalms*, focusing more directly on the original Hebrew while seeking a more inclusive final text of the sort preferred in the current worship of their respective communions.

We consulted with the undersecretary of the Congregation for Divine Worship and the Discipline of the Sacraments, who indicated that he considered the project a worthwhile endeavor, suggesting that it first be vetted by the US Conference of Catholic Bishops through their offices of Divine Worship and Ecumenical and Interreligious Affairs. These offices responded in the affirmative, stipulating that, while recognizing the value of the project as an ecumenical endeavor, it would be necessary to state clearly that *The Ecumenical Grail Psalter* is *not approved for liturgical use in the Catholic Church*, which retains for its liturgical use the original *Revised Grail Psalms* as approved by both the USCCB and the Congregation for Divine Worship and the Discipline of the Sacraments. Thus *The Ecumenical Grail Psalter* came to be.

At this point it must be admitted that an ecumenical edition of *The Revised Grail Psalms*, which strives for a nonexclusive text that avoids unnecessary gender-specific references to the Deity or to the human person in general terms, is necessarily going to have to admit some paraphrasis in its own rendering of the text into English. We have sought to strike a balance here, avoiding masculine terminology when referring to God wherever possible, and allowing gender-specific terms only when they refer directly to historical persons who are males. This includes those prophetic texts that have come to be associated with Jesus Christ in the tradition of interpretation. On the other had, it was our editorial decision to retain the literary use of the feminine pronoun when referring to Jerusalem (or other cities or comparable political entities; cf. Ps 46:6; 48:4,13–14; 68:32; 87:5; 102:15; 125:2; 132:15–16), to retain the association with historic and biblical custom of referring to such entities in the feminine, particularly as "daughter," as in "daughter Zion" and other such designations (cf. Ps 9:15; 73:28; also 45:13; 137:8).

A Word for Those Unfamiliar with the Book of Psalms

Every day, people are reading or hearing the Psalms for the first time. Some have told me that their first encounter from the Book of Psalms as a child or adolescent left them feeling that they did not understand it, and they never felt drawn back to it. Others are aware of the Psalms but simply have not read or prayed seriously with them. Yet interest in this biblical book of prayers continues to grow, and with good reason.

One effective way to appropriate the prayers and images of the Psalter is to use them to express one's own human need for God. So often we find ourselves in circumstances that compel us to communicate our situation to the Lord. As we slowly come to realize that all blessing is from God, we discover within ourselves the need to lift up words of praise and thanks to our Maker and Lord. In moments of sadness, disappointment, frustration, and even anger, almighty God is the one to whom we turn, hoping for a reversal of our troubled situation. In the Psalter are many such expressions of human need before God; making such prayers our own is the only way to become truly familiar with these prayers that people of faith have used for centuries both in moments of private appeal and in joyous community celebrations.

Below is a short list of different circumstances that frequently lead one to prayer. For each of these, we have suggested corresponding Psalms to give appropriate expression to these circumstances. It is our hope that this might open new avenues of satisfying and enriching prayer for newcomer to the Psalms. The list is not definitive, but meant rather to present some of the best-known and most frequently used Psalms under familiar headings; you will see that some Psalms are listed more than once.

1. A Morning Prayer—Psalms 3, 5, 63, 143
2. An Evening Prayer—Psalms 130, 141
3. A Night Prayer—Psalms 4, 91, 134
4. Praise of God—Psalms 8, 66, 104, 135, 136, 145, 148, 150
5. Thanksgiving to God—Psalms 30, 34, 92, 111, 116, 118, 138
6. Prayer for Upright Living—Psalms 1, 15, 24, 37, 112

7. Prayer for Forgiveness—Psalms 32, 51, 80, 86
8. Longing for Union with God—Psalms 12, 27, 42, 63, 139
9. The Vanity of Human Life—Psalms 39, 49, 73, 90
10. Laments to Life's Struggles—Psalms 22, 25, 31, 40, 90
11. Confidence in God—Psalms 4, 16, 23, 25, 46, 131, 139
12. Hymns about the Messiah—Psalms 2, 23, 45, 89, 110, 132
13. Prayer in Old Age—Psalms 71, 90, 139
14. Historical Psalms—Psalms 78, 105, 106, 135, 136
15. Prayer in Times of Danger—Psalms 7, 28, 35, 38, 54, 56, 140

The Church has always intended that the community's use of the Psalms in congregational prayer serve as a source of inspiration for personal prayer as well. Integral to the reflective appropriation of the Scriptures is to pray directly from the biblical text. When the congregation prays a psalm together, it serves as the voice of the whole community responding to the voice of God that they have heard in the other biblical readings. We can certainly make use of the same method when we pray the Psalms privately: reading the text of the psalm, reflecting on it, and then lifting up to God our own words that arise from our meditative encounter with the text.

Reading and praying in this manner, placing the texts of the Psalms at the heart of our prayer, we are formed in the spirit of the Bible's own prayer book. Whether in community prayer or in prayer of the heart alone in one's room, these ancient prayers of synagogue and church have taught generations of faith-filled people the way of redemption as it is lived out in everyday life. Their universal message continues to inspire people to open wide their hearts to a God whose word to us is "ever ancient, ever new," as Saint Augustine so aptly put it. The Psalms become our daily companion in prayer and our daily conversation with the living God, who has created us for just that purpose.

Acknowledgments

When this work of the revision of the 1963 Grail Psalms was undertaken in 1998, we had no idea how extensive an effort would be required to bring it to a successful conclusion. The work of the monks of Conception Abbey involved in producing the work beyond translation included proofreading, musical considerations, and computer layout, as well as suggestions to improve felicity of expression in both grammar and syntax of both the text and ancillary documents. And finally, it is worth noting that the monks of Conception Abbey prayed the texts of *The Revised Grail Psalms* for several years before the text was finalized, engaging them with heart and soul, and offering suggestions for improvement and words of encouragement for what we hoped would eventually emerge as yet one more contribution from the Benedictine Order to the ongoing growth and development of the Church's liturgy.

The three most recent popes have indicated their conviction that Benedictine monks are especially situated to engage in the important work of ecumenical and interreligious dialogue and prayer. The monks of Conception Abbey are honored to have been invited to participate in an endeavor that supports the ongoing ecumenical work of so many Christian communities, especially as it involves our shared prayer and the worship of the one God.

We offer our sincere thanks to all those who read through this translation and offered their suggestions and reactions. Various Christian communities were consulted in this endeavor in the hope that this translation would meet their needs, hopes, and expectations for an ecumenical psalter. We continue to hope that such will be the case. May God be praised in all ways and at all times.

Abbot Gregory J. Polan, OSB
Conception Abbey

BOOK ONE OF THE PSALTER

Psalm 1

[1] Bléssed indéed are thóse
who fóllow not the cóunsel of the wícked,
nor stánd in the páth with sínners,
nor abíde in the cómpany of scórners,
[2] but whose delíght is the láw of the Lórd,
and who pónder God's láw day and níght.

[3] Such péople are like trées that are plánted
besíde the flówing wáters,
that yíeld their frúit in due séason,
and whose léaves shall néver fáde;
and áll that they dó shall prósper.

[4] Not só are the wícked, not só!
For théy, like wínnowed cháff,
shall be dríven awáy by the wínd.

[5] When the wícked are júdged they shall not ríse,
nor shall sínners in the cóuncil of the ríghteous;
[6] for the Lord knóws the wáy of the ríghteous,
but the wáy of the wícked will pérish.

Psalm 2

[1] Whý do the nátions conspíre,
and the péoples plót in váin?
[2] They aríse, the rúlers of the éarth;
nobles plót against the Lórd and his Anóinted.
[3] "Let us búrst asúnder their fétters.
Let us cast óff from ús their cháins."

[4] The One who síts in the héavens láughs;
the Lórd derídes and mócks them.
[5] Then the Lórd will spéak in his ánger,
and stríke them with térror and ráge.
[6] "It is Í who have appóinted my kíng
on Zíon, my hóly móuntain."

[7] I will annóunce the decrée of the Lórd:
The Lord sáid to me, "Yóu are my Són.
It is Í who have begótten you this dáy."

[8] "Ásk of me and Í will make nátions your héritage,
and the énds of the éarth as your posséssion.
[9] With a ród of íron you will rúle them;
like a pótter's jár you will shátter them."

[10] So nów, O rúlers, understánd;
take wárning, nóbles of the éarth.
[11] Sérve the Lórd with féar;
exult with trémbling, páy your hómage,
[12] lest God be ángry and you pérish on the wáy
in the súdden bláze of God's ánger.

Blessed are áll who trúst in Gód!

Psalm 3

[1] *A Psalm of David as he is fleeing from his son Absalom.*

[2] How mány are my fóes, O Lórd!
How mány are rísing up agáinst me!
[3] How mány are sáying abóut me,
"There is nó salvátion for yóu in Gód."

[4] But yóu, Lord, are a shíeld abóut me,
my glóry, who líft up my héad.
[5] I crý alóud to the Lórd,
from whose hóly móuntain comes my ánswer.

[6] I lie dówn, I sléep and I wáke,
for the Lórd uphólds me.
[7] I will not féar even thóusands of péople
who are ránged on every síde agáinst me.

Aríse, Lord; sáve me, my Gód,
[8] you who stríke all my fóes on the chéek,
you who bréak the téeth of the wícked!
[9] Salvátion belóngs to the Lórd;
may your bléssing bé on your péople!

Psalm 4

[1] *For the Choirmaster. With stringed instruments.*
A Psalm of David.

[2] O Gód of my ríghteousness, give ánswer when I cáll;
from ánguish you reléased me, have mércy, hear my práyer!

[3] O you péople, how lóng will my glóry be dishónored,
will you lóve what is fútile and séek what is fálse?

[4] Knów that the Lórd works wónders for the fáithful;
the Lórd will héar me whenéver I call óut.

[5] Tremble, dó not sin: pónder on your béd and be stíll.
[6] Offer a ríghteous sácrifice, and trúst in the Lórd.

[7] "O that wé might sée better tímes" many sáy.
Lift up the líght of your fáce on ús, O Lórd.

[8] You have pút into my héart a gréater jóy
than abúndance of gráin and new wíne can províde.

[9] In péace I will lie dówn and fall asléep,
for yóu alone, O Lórd, make me dwéll in sáfety.

Psalm 5

[1] *For the Choirmaster. With flutes. A Psalm of David.*

[2] To my wórds give éar, O Lórd;
give héed to my síghs.
[3] Atténd to the sóund of my crý,
my Sóvereign and my Gód.

[4] To yóu do I práy, O Lórd.
In the mórning you héar my vóice;
in the mórning I pléad and watch befóre you.

[5] You are no Gód who delíghts in évil;
no sínner is your guést.
[6] The bóastful shall not stánd before your éyes.

[7] Áll who do évil you despíse;
all who líe you destróy.
Whoéver speaks líes and sheds blóod
the Lórd detésts.

[8] Yet through the gréatness of your fáithful lóve,
I énter your hóuse.
I bow dówn before your hóly témple,
in áwe of yóu.

[9] Léad me, LÓRD, in your ríghteousness,
because of my fóes;
make stráight your wáy befóre me.

[10] No trúth can be fóund in their móuths,
their héart is all málice,
their thróat a wide-ópen gráve;
with their tóngue they flátter.

[11] Decláre them guílty, O Gód.
Let them fáil in their desígns.
Drive them óut for their mány transgréssions,
for against yóu have they rebélled.

[12] All who take réfuge in yóu shall be glád,
and ever crý out their jóy.
You shélter them; in yóu they rejóice,
those who lóve your náme.
[13] It is yóu who bless the ríghteous, O LÓRD,
you surróund them with your fávor like a shíeld.

Psalm 6

[1] *For the Choirmaster. With stringed instruments,*
upon the Eighth Chord. A Psalm of David.

[2] O Lórd, do not rebúke me in your ánger;
repróve me nót in your ráge.
[3] Have mércy on me, Lórd, for I lánguish.
Lord, héal me; my bónes are sháking,
[4] and my sóul is gréatly sháken.

But yóu, O Lórd, how lóng?
[5] Retúrn, Lord, réscue my sóul.
Sáve me in your grácious lóve.
[6] For in déath there is nó remémbrance of yóu;
whó can give you práise from Shéol?

[7] Í am exháusted with my gróaning;
every níght I drench my béd with téars,
I bedéw my cóuch with wéeping.
[8] My éyes waste awáy with gríef;
they have grown wéak surróunded by áll my fóes.

[9] Léave me, áll who do évil,
for the Lord héeds the sóund of my wéeping.
[10] The Lórd has héard my pléa;
The Lórd will recéive my práyer.
[11] All my fóes will be shámed and greatly sháken,
súddenly pút to sháme.

Psalm 7

[1] *A Lament of David that he chanted to the LORD on account of Cush, the Benjaminite.*

[2] O LORD, my Gód, I take réfuge in yóu.
Save and réscue me from áll my pursúers,
[3] lest like a líon they téar me apárt,
and drag me óff with nó one to réscue me.

[4] If I have dóne this, O LÓRD, my Gód,
if thére is wróng on my hánds,
[5] if I have páid back évil for góod,
or plúndered my fóe without cáuse:

[6] Then let my fóes pursúe my soul and séize me,
let them trámple my lífe to the gróund,
and láy my hónor in the dúst.

[7] O LÓRD, rise úp in your ánger;
be exálted in your fúry toward my fóes.
Awáke for me the jústice you have órdered.
[8] Let the cómpany of péoples gather róund you,
as you táke your seat abóve them on hígh.

[9] The LÓRD is júdge of the péoples.
Give júdgment for mé, O LÓRD,
for I am ríghteous and blámeless of héart.

[10] Put an énd to the évil of the wícked!
Make the ríghteous stand fírm.
It is yóu who test mínd and héart,
O ríghteous Gód!

[11] Gód is a shíeld befóre me,
who sáves the úpright of héart.
[12] God is a júdge, just and pówerful and pátient,
not éxercising ánger every dáy.

[13] Against sómeone who does nót repént,
Gód will shárpen a swórd,
bénd a bów and make réady.
[14] For such a óne God prepáres deadly wéapons,
bárbing árrows with fíre.

[15] Here are the ónes who concéive iníquity,
pregnant with málice, giving bírth to líes.
[16] They díg a pít and bóre it déep,
and in the tráp they have máde they fáll.
[17] For their málice recóils on their own héads;
on their own skúlls their víolence fálls.

[18] I thánk the Lórd for divine ríghteousness,
and síng to the náme of the Lórd, the Most
Hígh.

Psalm 8

[1] *For the Choirmaster. Upon the* gittith. *A Psalm of David.*

[2] O LÓRD, our Sóvereign, how majéstic
is your náme through áll the éarth!

Your májesty is sét above the héavens.
[3] From the móuths of chíldren and of bábes
you fáshioned praise to fóil your énemy,
to sílence the fóe and the rébel.

[4] When I sée the héavens, the wórk of your fíngers,
the móon and the stárs which you arránged,
[5] what are húman béings that you kéep them in mínd,
mortal créatures that you cáre for thém?

[6] Yet you have máde them little lówer than the ángels;
with glóry and hónor you crówned them,
[7] gave them pówer over the wórks of your hánds:
you put áll things únder their féet,

[8] Áll of them, shéep and óxen,
yes, éven the cáttle of the fíelds,
[9] birds of the áir, and físh of the séa
that máke their wáy through the séas.

[10] O LÓRD, our Sóvereign, how majéstic
is your náme through áll the éarth!

Psalm 9

[1] *For the Choirmaster. In the manner of a Chant*
Mut Labben. *A Psalm of David.*

[2] I will práise you, Lórd, with all my héart;
all your wónders Í will recóunt.
[3] I will rejóice in yóu and be glád,
and sing psálms to your náme, O Most Hígh.

[4] Sée how my énemies turn báck,
how they stúmble and pérish befóre you.
[5] You uphéld the jústice of my cáuse;
you sat enthróned, júdging with ríghteousness.

[6] You have rebúked the nátions, destróyed the wícked;
you have wíped out their náme forév er and éver.
[7] The fóe is destróyed, etérnally rúined.
You uprόoted their cíties; their mémory has
pérished.

[8] But the Lórd sits enthróned forév er,
and has sét up a thróne for júdgment.
[9] God will júdge the wórld with ríghteousness,
and will góvern the péoples with équity.

[10] For the oppréssed, the Lórd will be a strónghold,
a strónghold in tímes of distréss.
[11] Those who knów your náme will trúst you;
you will nót forsáke those who séek you, O Lórd.

[12] Sing psálms to the Lórd who dwells in Zíon,
whose mighty wórks are revéaled among the
péoples,
[13] for the Avénger of Blóod has remémbered them,
has not forgótten the crý of the póor.

[14] Have mércy on mé, O Lórd;
sée how I súffer from my fóes,
you who ráise me from the gátes of déath,
[15] that Í may recóunt all your práise
at the gátes of dáughter Zíon,
and rejóice in yóur salvátion.

[16] The nátions have fállen in the pít which they
máde;
their féet have been cáught in the snáre they láid.
[17] The Lórd is knówn for the júdgment enácted.
The wícked are snáred by the wórk of their
hánds.

[18] Let the wícked go dówn to Shéol,
all the nátions forgétful of Gód:
[19] for the néedy shall not álways be forgótten,
nor the hópes of the póor ever pérish.

[20] Arise, O Lórd, let human stréngth not prevá il!
Let the nátions be júdged befóre you.
[21] Stríke them with térror, O Lórd;
let the nátions knów they are ónly húman.

Psalm 10 *(9:22–39)*

[1] Whý, O Lórd, do you stánd far óff,
and híde yoursélf in tímes of distréss?
[2] The póor are devóured by the príde of the wícked;
they are cáught in the schémes that óthers have
máde.

[3] For the wícked bóast of their sóuls' desíres;
the cóvetous blasphéme and spúrn the Lórd.
[4] The wicked sáy with príde, "Gód will not púnish.
There ís no Gód." Súch are their thóughts.

[5] Their páth is éver untróubled;
your júdgments are on hígh, far remóved.
All thóse who oppóse them, they deríde.
[6] In their héarts they think, "Néver shall we fálter;
néver shall misfórtune be our lót."

[7] Their móuths are full of cúrsing, guíle, oppréssion;
únder their tóngues are decéit and évil.
[8] They sít in ámbush in the víllages;
in hidden pláces, they múrder the ínnocent.

The éyes of the wícked keep wátch for the
hélpless.
[9] They lúrk in híding like líons in their láirs;
they lúrk in híding to séize the póor,
they séize the póor and dráw them to their nét.

[10] They cróuch, prepáring to spríng,
and the hélpless fall préy to their stréngth.
[11] They sáy in their héarts, "God forgéts,
turns awáy from us, and néver sees a thíng."

[12] Arise, O Lórd; lift up your hánd, O Gód!
Do nót forgét the póor!
[13] Whý should the wícked spurn Gód,
and sáy in their héarts, "You will not cáll us to
accóunt"?

[14] But you have séen the tróuble and sórrow.
You nóte it; you táke it in your hánds.
The hélpless one relíes on yóu,
for yóu are the hélper of the órphan.

[15] Break the árm of the wícked and the sínner!
Pursue their wíckedness till nóthing remáins!
[16] The Lord is Sóvereign foréver and éver.
Nations shall pérish from the lánd of the Lórd.

[17] O Lórd, you have héard the desíre of the póor.
You stréngthen their héarts; you túrn your éar
[18] to gíve right júdgment for the órphan and
oppréssed,
so that nó one on éarth may strike térror agáin.

Psalm 11 (10)

[1] *For the Choirmaster. Of David.*

In the Lórd I have táken réfuge.
Hów can you sáy to my sóul,
"Flý like a bírd to the móuntain!

[2] "Look, the wícked are bénding their bów!
They are fíxing their árrow on the stríng,
to shoot the úpright of héart in the dárk.
[3] Foundátions ónce destróyed,
whát can the ríghteous dó?"

[4] The Lórd is in his hóly témple;
in héaven is the thróne of the Lórd,
whose éyes behóld the wórld,
whose gáze inspécts the human ráce.

[5] The Lord inspécts the ríghteous and the wícked,
and hátes the lóver of víolence,
[6] sending fíre and brímstone on the wícked,
a scorching wínd to fill their cúp.
[7] For the Lórd is ríghteous and lóves righteous
déeds;
the úpright shall behóld the face of Gód.

Psalm 12 *(11)*

[1] *For the Choirmaster. Upon the Eighth Chord.*
A Psalm of David.

[2] Save me, O Lórd, for the hóly ones áre no móre;
the fáithful have vánished from the húman ráce.
[3] They bábble vánities, óne to anóther,
with cúnning líps, with divíded héart.

[4] May the Lórd destróy all cúnning líps,
the tóngue that útters bóastful wórds,
[5] Thóse who sáy, "We preváil with our tóngue;
our líps are our ówn, whó can commánd us?"

[6] "For the póor who are oppréssed and the néedy
who sígh,
nów will Í aríse," says the Lórd;
"I will gránt them the salvátion for whích they
lóng."
[7] The wórds of the Lórd are wórds without álloy,
sílver from the fúrnace, séven times refíned.

[8] It is yóu, O Lórd, who will kéep us sáfe,
and protéct us foréver from thís generátion.
[9] The wícked prówl on évery síde,
while báseness is exálted by the húman ráce.

Psalm 13 *(12)*

[1] *For the Choirmaster. A Psalm of David.*

[2] How lóng, O Lórd? Will you forgét me forévér?
How lóng will you híde your fáce from mé?
[3] How lóng must I bear gríef in my sóul,
have sórrow in my héart all day lóng?
How lóng shall my énemy prevàil over mé?

[4] Look, ánswer mé, O Lórd my Gód!
Give líght to my éyes lest I fáll asleep in déath;
[5] lest my énemy sáy, "I have preváiled over yóu;"
lest my fóes rejóice when they sée me fáll.

[6] As for mé, I trúst in your fáithful lóve.
Let my héart rejóice in yóur salvátion.
[7] I will síng to the Lórd who has been bóuntiful
with mé.

Psalm 14 *(13)*

[1] *For the Choirmaster. A Psalm of David.*

The fóolish have sáid in their héarts,
"There ís no Gód."
Their déeds are corrúpt, depráved;
no one dóes any góod.

[2] The LÓRD looks dówn from héaven
on the húman ráce,
to sée if ány are wíse,
if ány seek Gód.

[3] Áll have góne astráy,
depráved, every óne;
there is nó one who dóes any góod;
nó, not even óne.

[4] Do nóne of the évildoers únderstánd?
They eat úp my péople as if éating bréad;
they néver call óut to the LÓRD.

[5] Thére they shall trémble with féar,
for Gód is with the ríghteous generátion.
[6] You may móck the pláns of the póor,
but their réfuge is the LÓRD.

[7] Oh, that the réscue of Ísrael might cóme from
Zíon.
When the LÓRD brings abóut the péople's retúrn,
then Jácob will be glád and Ísrael rejóice.

Psalm 15 *(14)*

[1] *A Psalm of David.*

Lord, whó may abíde in your tént,
and dwéll on your hóly móuntain?

[2] Whoéver wálks without fáult;
who dóes what is ríghteous,
and spéaks with héartfelt trúth.

[3] Whoéver does not slánder with the tóngue;
who dóes no wróng to a néighbor,
who cásts no slúr on a fríend,
[4] who lóoks with scórn on the wícked,
but hónors those who féar the Lórd.

Whoever kéeps an oath, whatéver the cóst,
[5] who lénds no móney at ínterest,
and accépts no bríbes against the ínnocent.

Such a óne shall néver be sháken.

Psalm 16 *(15)*

[1] *A* Miktam. *Of David.*

Presérve me, O Gód, for in yóu I take réfuge.
[2] I sáy to the Lórd, "You are my Lórd.
Yóu are my góod, you alóne."

[3] As for the hóly ones who dwéll in the lánd,
they are nóble, and in thém I delíght.
[4] Those who chóose other góds incréase their
sórrows.
I will nót take párt in their ófferings of blóod.
Nór will I táke their námes upon my líps.

[5] O Lórd, it is yóu who are my pórtion and cúp;
it is yóu yoursélf who secúre my déstiny.
[6] Pléasant pláces are márked out for mé:
a fair héritage indéed is my lót!

[7] I will bléss the Lórd who gíves me cóunsel,
who éven at níght diréects my héart.
[8] I kéep the Lórd befóre me álways;
with Gód at my ríght hand, I shall nót be móved.

[9] And so my héart rejóices, my sóul is glád;
éven my bódy shall rést in sáfety.
[10] For yóu will not abándon my sóul to Shéol,
nor lét your hóly one sée corrúption.

[11] You will shów me the páth of lífe,
the fúllness of jóy in your présence,
at your ríght hand, blíss foréver.

Psalm 17 *(16)*

[1] *A Prayer of David.*

O Lórd, hear a cáuse that is júst,
pay héed to my crý.
Túrn your éar to my práyer:
no decéit is on my líps.
[2] From yóu may my jústice come fórth.
Your eyes discérn what is úpright.

[3] Search my héart and vísit me by níght.
Test me by fíre, and you will fínd no wrong in mé.

[4] My móuth does not transgréss as others dó;
on accóunt of the wórds of your líps,
I have avóided the páths of the víolent.

[5] I képt my steps fírmly in your páths.
My féet have néver fáltered.

[6] To you I cáll; for you will súrely héed me, O Gód.
Túrn your éar to me; héar my wórds.
[7] Displáy your fáithful lóve,
yóu who delíver from their fóes
those who trúst in yóur right hánd.

[8] Guárd me as the ápple of your éye.
Híde me in the shádow of your wíngs
[9] from the víolent attáck of the wícked.

My foes encírcle me with déadly intént.
[10] Their hearts tight shút, their móuths speak próudly.
[11] They advánce agáinst me, and nów they surróund me.
Their eyes wátch to stríke me to the gróund.
[12] They are like a líon réady to cláw,
like some young líon cróuched in híding.

[13] Arise, O Lórd, confrónt them, stríke them dówn!
Let your swórd delíver my sóul from the wícked!
[14] Let your hánd, O Lórd, delíver me
from those whose pórtion in lífe is of this wórld.

May what yóu have stored úp for them fill their béllies;
may their óffspring be sáted with its plénty,
and let them léave what is léft for their yóung.
[15] As for mé, I shall behóld your fáce in ríghteousness;
when I awáke I shall be filled with the vísion of your présence.

Psalm 18 *(17)*

[1] *For the Choirmaster. Of David, the servant of the Lord, who spoke the words of this canticle to the Lord when he had been freed from the power of all his enemies and from the hand of Saul.*
[2] *He said:*

I lóve you, Lórd, my stréngth;
[3] O Lord, my róck, my fórtress, my sávior;
my Gód, my róck where I take réfuge;
my shíeld, my saving stréngth, my strónghold.
[4] I cry óut, "O práised be the Lórd!"
and sée, I am sáved from my fóes.

[5] The wáves of déath rose abóut me;
the tórrents of destrúction assáiled me;
[6] the snáres of Shéol surróunded me;
the tráps of déath confrónted me.

[7] In my ánguish I cálled to the Lórd;
I críed to my Gód for hélp.
In the héavenly témple my vóice was héard;
my crýing réached God's éars.

[8] The éarth then réeled and rócked;
the móuntains were sháken to their báse,
quáking at the ánger of Gód,

[9] from whose nóstrils cáme forth smóke,
from whose móuth came scórching fíre;
from thís live cóals were kíndled.

[10] God bént the héavens and came dówn,
a clóud of thick dárkness benéath,
[11] ríding on a chérub in flíght;
sóaring on the wíngs of the wínd.

[12] The dárkness sérved as a cóvering,
the dark wáters of the clóuds as a tént.
[13] A bríghtness shone óut before the Lórd,
with háilstones and fláshes of fíre.

[14] The Lórd then thúndered in the héavens;
amid háil and cóals of fíre
the vóice of the Most Hígh rang fórth.
[15] Shooting árrows, scáttering the fóe,
flashing líghtnings, God pút them to flíght.

[16] The béd of the ócean was revéaled;
the foundátions of the wórld were laid báre
at yóur rebúke, O Lórd,
at the blást of the bréath of your nóstrils.

[17] From on hígh God reached dówn and séized me,
drew me fórth from the míghty wáters,
[18] and sáved me from my pówerful fóe,
from my énemies, whose stréngth I could not mátch.

[19] They assáiled me in the dáy of my misfórtune,
but the LÓRD was my stróng suppórt,
[20] bringing me óut to a pláce of fréedom,
sáving me, indéed, with delíght.

[21] The LORD rewárded me becáuse I was ríghteous,
repáid me, for my hánds were cléan,
[22] for I have képt the wáys of the LÓRD,
and have not fállen awáy from my Gód.

[23] For befóre me are áll the júdgments of Gód,
whose commánds I have not cást asíde.
[24] Í have been blámeless befóre the Almíghty;
I have képt mysélf from guílt.
[25] You repáid me, O LÓRD, for I was ríghteous,
and my hánds were cléan in your síght.

[26] With the fáithful you shów yourself fáithful;
with the blámeless you shów yourself blámeless.
[27] With the sincére you shów yourself sincére,
but the cúnning you outdó in shréwdness;
[28] for you sáve a lówly péople,
but bring lów the éyes that are próud.

[29] It is yóu who give líght to my lámp;
the LÓRD my God líghtens my dárkness.
[30] With yóu I can crúsh the fóe,
with my Gód I can scále a wáll.

[31] The wáy of Gód is blámeless;
the wórd of the Lórd is púre;
God is a shíeld for áll who trúst.

[32] For whó is Gód but the Lórd?
Whó is a róck but our Gód?
[33] It is Gód who gírds me with stréngth,
and kéeps my páth free of bláme,
[34] Made my féet as swíft as the déer's,
áble to stand fírm on the héights.

[35] God has tráined my hánds for báttle,
and my árms to bénd the bronze bów.
[36] You gáve me your sáving shíeld;
with your right hánd, you gáve me suppórt;
you bent dówn to máke me gréat.
[37] You léngthened my stéps benéath me;
and my féet have néver slípped.

[38] I pursúed and overtóok my fóes,
néver turning báck till they were sláin.
[39] I strúck them so they cóuld not ríse;
they féll benéath my féet.

[40] You gírded me with stréngth for báttle;
you made my énemies fáll benéath me.
[41] You máde my fóes take flíght;
those who háted me Í destróyed.

[42] They cried óut, but there was nó one to sáve
them,
cried to the Lórd, who díd not ánswer.
[43] I crúshed them fine as dúst before the wínd,
trod them dówn like dírt in the stréets.

[44] From the féuds of the péople you delívered me,
and pút me at the héad of the nátions.
Péople unknówn to me sérved me;
[45] when they héard of mé, they obéyed me.

Foreign nátions cáme to me crínging;
[46] foreign nátions fáded awáy.
Trémbling, they came fórth from their
strónghholds.

[47] The Lord líves, and blést be my Róck!
May the Gód of my salvátion be exálted,
[48] the Gód who gíves me redréss
and subdúes the péoples únder me.

[49] You sáved me from my fúrious fóes;
you sét me abóve my assáilants;
you sáved me from the víolent óne.
[50] So I will práise you, LÓRD, among the nátions;
to your náme will I síng a psálm.

[51] The LORD gíves great víctories to the kíng,
and shows grácious lóve for the anóinted one,
for Dávid and his prógeny foréver.

Psalm 19 *(18)*

[1] *For the Choirmaster. A Psalm of David.*

[2] The héavens declâre the glóry of Gód,
whose hándiwork the fírmament procláims.
[3] Dáy unto dáy convéys the méssage,
and níght unto níght impárts the knówledge.

[4] No spéech, no wórd, whose vóice goes unhéeded;
[5] their sóund goes fórth through áll the éarth,
their méssage to the útmost bóunds of the wórld.

[6] There Gód has pláced a tént for the sún;
it comes fórth like a brídegroom cóming from his
tént,
rejóices like a chámpion to rún its cóurse.

[7] At one énd of the héavens is the rísing of the sún;
to its fúrthest énd it rúns its cóurse.
There is nóthing concéaled from its búrning héat.

* * *

[8] The láw of the Lórd is pérfect;
it revíves the sóul.
The decrées of the Lórd are stéadfast;
they give wísdom to the símple.

[9] The précepts of the Lórd are ríght;
they gládden the héart.
The commánd of the Lórd is cléar;
it gives líght to the éyes.

[10] The féar of the Lórd is púre,
abíding foréver.
The júdgments of the Lórd are trúe;
they are, áll of them, ríghteous.

[11] They are móre to be desíred than góld,
than quántities of góld.
And swéeter are théy than hóney,
than honey flówing from the cómb.

[12] So in thém your sérvant finds instrúction;
great rewárd is in their kéeping.
[13] But whó can detéct their own érrors?
From hídden faults acquít me.

[14] From presúmption restráin your sérvant;
máy it not rúle me.
Thén shall Í be blámeless,
cléan from grave sín.

[15] May the spóken wórds of my móuth,
the thóughts of my héart,
win fávor in your síght, O Lórd,
my róck and my redéemer!

Psalm 20 *(19)*

[1] *For the Choirmaster. A Psalm of David.*

[2] May the Lord ánswer you in tíme of tríal;
may the náme of Jacob's Gód protéct you,
[3] sénding you hélp from the hóly place,
and gíving you suppórt from Zíon.

[4] May God remémber áll your ófferings,
recéive your sácrifice with fávor,
[5] gíve you your héart's desíre,
and fulfíll every óne of your pláns.

[6] May we ríng out our jóy at your víctory,
and raise bánners in the náme of our Gód.
May the Lórd grant áll your práyers.

[7] Now I knów the anóinted one is sáved by the Lórd,
who ánswers from the hóly héavens
with the right hánd of víctory and míght.

[8] Sóme put their trúst in cháriots or hórses,
but wé in the náme of the Lórd, our Gód.
[9] Théy will cóllapse and fáll,
but wé shall rise úp and hold fírm.
[10] Grant salvátion to the kíng, O Lórd,
give ánswer on the dáy we cáll.

Psalm 21 (20)

[1] *For the Choirmaster. A Psalm of David.*

[2] In your stréngth, O Lórd, the kíng rejóices;
how gréatly your salvátion mákes him glád!
[3] You have gránted his héart's desíre;
you have nót withhéld the práyer of his líps.

[4] You cáme to méet him with bléssings of
prospérity;
you have sét on his héad a crówn of pure góld.
[5] He ásked you for lífe and thís you have gíven:
dáys that will lást from áge to áge.

[6] In your salvátion how gréat is his glóry;
you have bestówed upon him májesty and
spléndor;
[7] you have gránted him bléssings forévér,
made him rejóice with the jóy of your fáce.

[8] The kíng has pláced his trúst in the Lórd,
through the lóve of the Most Hígh is unshákén.

[9] Your hánd will find óut all your fóes,
your right hánd will find óut those who háte you.
[10] You will búrn them like a blázing fúrnace
on the dáy when yóu appéar,
and the Lórd will consúme them in ánger:
fíre will swállow them úp.

[11] You will wípe out their descéndants from the
éarth,
and their óffspring from the húman ráce.
[12] Thóugh they planned évil agáinst you,
though they plótted, they shall nót preváil.

[13] For yóu will fórce them to retréat;
at thém you will áim with your bów.
[14] O Lórd, aríse in your stréngth;
we shall síng and práise your pówer.

***Psalm 22** (21)*

[1] *For the Choirmaster. In the manner of "The Doe at Daybreak." A Psalm of David.*

[2] My God, my Gód, whý have you forsáken me?
Why are you fár from sáving mé,
so fár from my wórds of ánguish?
[3] O my Gód, I call by dáy and you dó not ánswer;
I cáll by níght and I fínd no relíef.

[4] Yet yóu, O Gód, are hóly,
enthróned on the práises of Ísrael.
[5] In you our áncestors pút their trúst;
they trústed and you sét them frée.
[6] When they críed to yóu, they escáped;
in you they trústed and were nót put to sháme.

[7] But Í am a wórm, not even húman,
scorned by éveryone, despísed by the péople.
[8] Áll who sée me deríde me;
they curl their líps, they sháke their héads:
[9] "You trústed in the LÓRD, may you nów be sáved,
yes, reléased, for in yóu God delíghts."

[10] Yes, it was yóu who tóok me from the wómb,
kept me sáfe on my móther's bréast.
[11] To yóu I was commítted from bírth;
from my móther's womb, yóu have been my Gód.
[12] Stáy not fár from mé;
trouble is néar, and there is nó one to hélp.

[13] Mány búlls have surróunded me,
fíerce búlls of Báshan close me ín.
[14] Agáinst me they ópen wide their móuths,
like a líon, rénding and róaring.

[15] Like wáter Í am poured óut,
disjóinted are áll my bónes.
My héart has becóme like wáx,
it is mélted withín my bréast.

[16] Párched as burnt cláy is my thróat,
my tóngue holds fást to my jáws.
You láy me in the dúst of déath.
[17] For dógs have surróunded mé;
a bánd of the wícked beséts me.
They tear hóles in my hánds and my féet;

[18] I can cóunt every óne of my bónes.
They stáre at mé and glóat.
[19] They divíde my clóthing amóng them,
cásting lóts for my róbe.

[20] But you, O Lórd, do not stáy far óff;
my stréngth, make háste to hélp me!
[21] Réscue my sóul from the swórd,
my lífe from the gríp of the dóg.
[22] Save my lífe from the jáws of the líon,
my poor sóul from the hórns of wild búlls.

[23] I will téll of your náme to my kín,
and práise you in the mídst of the assémbly:
[24] "Yóu who fear the LÓRD, give práise;
all óffspring of Jácob, give glóry;
offer réverence, all you óffspring of Ísrael.

[25] For the Almíghty has néver despísed
nor scórned the póverty of the póor.
From the póor God's fáce is not hídden;
they were héard whenéver they críed."

[26] Yóu are my práise in the gréat assémbly.
My vóws I will páy before thóse who fear the Lórd.
[27] The póor shall éat and shall háve their fíll.
They shall práise the LORD, thóse who séek our
Gód.
May your héarts live ón foréver and éver!

[28] All the éarth shall remémber and retúrn to the
LÓRD.
All fámilies of the nátions wórship and bow
dówn,
[29] for the kíngdom is the LÓRD's, who is rúler of the
nátions.
[30] They shall éat and adóre, all who sléep in the
éarth;
before the Lórd shall bów all who go dówn to the
dúst.

[31] And my sóul shall líve for God, my óffspring too
shall sérve.
To generátions yet to cóme they shall téll of the
LÓRD,
[32] decláre delíverance to péoples yet unbórn:
"Thése are the thíngs the LÓRD has dóne."

Psalm 23 (22)

[1] *A Psalm of David.*

The Lórd is my shépherd;
there is nóthing I shall wánt.
[2] Frésh and gréen are the pástures
where you gíve me repóse.
Near réstful wáters you léad me;
[3] to revíve my sóul.

You guíde me alóng the right páth,
for the sáke of your náme.
[4] Though I should wálk in the válley of the shádow
of déath,
no évil would I féar, for you are wíth me.
Your cróok and your stáff will give me cómfort.

[5] You have prepáred a táble befóre me
in the síght of my fóes.
My héad you have anóinted with óil;
my cúp is overflówing.

[6] Surely góodness and kíndness shall fóllow me
all the dáys of my lífe.
In the Lórd's own hóuse shall I dwéll
for léngth of days unénding.

Psalm 24 *(23)*

[1] *A Psalm of David.*

The Lórd's is the éarth and its fúllness,
the wórld, and thóse who dwéll in it.
[2] It is the Lórd who sét it on the séas,
and máde it fírm on the rívers.

[3] Who shall clímb the móuntain of the Lórd?
Who shall stánd in God's hóly pláce?
[4] The clean of hánds and púre of héart,
whose sóuls are not sét on vain thíngs,
who have not swórn decéitful wórds.

[5] Bléssings from the Lórd shall they recéive,
and right rewárd from the Gód who sáves them.
[6] Such are the péople who séek the Lórd,
who seek the fáce of the Gód of Jácob.

* * *

[7] O gátes, lift hígh your héads;
grow hígher, áncient dóors.
Let the kíng of glóry énter!

[8] Whó is this kíng of glóry?
The Lórd, the míghty, the váliant;
the Lórd, the váliant in wár.

[9] O gátes, lift hígh your héads;
grow hígher, áncient dóors.
Let the kíng of glóry énter!

[10] Whó is this kíng of glóry?
The Lórd of héavenly hósts;
thís is the kíng of glóry.

Psalm 25 *(24)*

[1] *Of David.*

To you, O Lórd, I líft up my sóul.
[2] In yóu, O my Gód, I have trústed;
let me nót be pút to sháme;
let not my énemies exúlt over mé.
[3] Let none who hópe in yóu be put to sháme;
but shámed are those who wántonly break fáith.

[4] O Lórd, make me knów your wáys.
Téach me your páths.
[5] Guíde me in your trúth, and téach me;
for yóu are the Gód of my salvátion.
I have hóped in yóu all day lóng.

[6] Remémber your compássion, O Lórd,
and your grácious lóve,
for théy are from of óld.

[7] Do not remémber the síns of my yóuth,
nor mý transgréssions.
In your grácious lóve remémber me,
becáuse of your góodness, O Lórd.

[8] Góod and úpright is the Lórd,
who therefore shóws the wáy to sínners,
[9] who guídes the húmble in right júdgment;
who téaches God's wáy to the húmble.

[10] All the páths of the Lórd are gracious lóve and
fáithfulness,
for those who kéep the commánds of the
cóvenant.
[11] O Lórd, for the sáke of your náme,
forgíve my guílt, for it is gréat.

[12] Who are théy that féar the Lórd?
God will shów them the páth to chóose.
[13] Their sóuls shall líve in háppiness,
and their descéndants shall posséss the lánd.
[14] The friéndship of the Lórd is for thóse who fear
Gód;
to thém is revéaled the cóvenant.

[15] My éyes are álways on the Lórd,
who réscues my féet from the snáre.
[16] Turn to mé and have mércy on mé,
for Í am alóne and póor.

[17] Relíeve the ánguish of my héart,
and sét me frée from my distréss.
[18] Sée my lówliness and súffering,
and táke away áll my síns.

[19] Sée how mány are my fóes:
with a víolent hátred they háte me.
[20] Presérve my lífe and réscue me.
Let me nót be pút to sháme,
for in yóu I take réfuge.

[21] May intégrity and vírtue protéct me,
for I have hóped in yóu, O Lórd.
[22] Grant redémption to Ísrael, O Gód,
from áll its distréss.

Psalm 26 *(25)*

[1] *Of David.*

Give júdgment for mé, O Lórd,
for Í have wálked in my intégrity.
I have trústed in the Lórd; I have not wávered.

[2] Exámine me, Lórd, and trý me.
O tést my héart and my mínd.
[3] Your faithful lóve is befóre my éyes,
and I wálk accórding to your trúth.

[4] I néver take my séat with líars,
and with hýpocrites I shäll not gó.
[5] I háte the évildoer's cómpany;
I will not táke my séat with the wícked.

[6] I wásh my hánds in ínnocence
and táke my pláce around your áltar,
[7] sínging a sóng of thanksgíving,
recóunting áll your wónders.
[8] O Lórd, I love the hóuse where you dwéll,
the pláce where your glóry abídes.

[9] Do not swéep away my sóul with sínners,
nor my lífe with thóse who shed blóod,
[10] in whose hánds are évil plóts,
whose right hánds are fílled with a bríbe.

[11] As for mé, I wálk in my intégrity.
Redéem me and have mércy on mé.
[12] My fóot stands on lével gróund:
I will bléss the LÓRD in the assémbly.

Psalm 27 (26)

[1] *Of David.*

The LÓRD is my líght and my salvátion;
whóm shall I féar?
The LÓRD is the strónghold of my lífe;
whóm should I dréad?

[2] When thóse who do évil draw néar
to devóur my flésh,
it is théy, my énemies and fóes,
who stúmble and fáll.

[3] Though an ármy encámp agáinst me,
my héart would not féar.
Though wár break óut agáinst me,
even thén would I trúst.

[4] There is óne thing I ásk of the LÓRD,
only thís do I séek:
to líve in the hóuse of the LÓRD
all the dáys of my lífe,
to gáze on the béauty of the LÓRD,
to inquíre at his témple.

[5] For thére I am sáfely shéltered
in the dáy of évil;
God hídes me under cóver of a tént;
sétting me hígh upon a róck.

[6] And nów my héad shall be ráised
above my fóes who surróund me,
and I shall óffer withín God's tént
sácrifices fúll of exultátion.
I will síng and make músic for the LÓRD.

[7] O LÓRD, hear my vóice when I cáll;
have mércy and ánswer me.
[8] Of yóu my héart has spóken,
"Séek the face of Gód."

It is your fáce, O LÓRD, that I séek;
[9] hide not your fáce from mé.
Dismíss not your sérvant in ánger;
yóu have been my hélp.

Dó not abándon or forsáke me,
O Gód, my Sávior!
[10] Though fáther and móther forsáke me,
the LÓRD will recéive me.

[11] Instrúct me, LÓRD, in your wáy;
on an éven path léad me
becáuse of my énemies.
[12] Do not léave me to the wíll of my fóes,
for false wítnesses rise úp agáinst me,
and they bréathe out víolence.

[13] I belíeve I shall sée the góodness of the LÓRD
in the lánd of the líving.
[14] Wáit for the LÓRD; be stróng;
be stouthéarted, and wáit for the LÓRD!

Psalm 28 (27)

[1] *Of David.*

To yóu, O Lórd, I cáll;
my róck, be not déaf to mé.
I shall go dówn to thóse in the pít,
if yóu are sílent to mé.

[2] Héar the vóice of my pléading
as I cáll to you for hélp,
as I líft up my hánds in práyer
to your hóly pláce.

[3] Do not drág me awáy with the wícked,
with thóse who do évil,
who speak wórds of péace to their néighbors,
but with málice in their héarts.

[4] Repáy them accórding to their déeds,
accórding to the évil of their áctions.
Accórding to their hándiwork, repáy them;
rénder them their dúe rewárd.

[5] For they ignóre your déeds, O LÓRD,
and the wórk of your hánds.
May you rúin them and néver rebuíld them.
[6] Blést be the LÓRD, who has héard
the sóund of my appéal.

[7] The LÓRD is my stréngth and my shíeld;
in Gód my heart trústs.
I was hélped; my héart rejóices,
and I práise God with my sóng.

[8] The LÓRD is the stréngth of the péople,
a saving réfuge for Gód's anóinted.
[9] Save your péople and bléss your héritage.
Shépherd them and cárry them forévér.

Psalm 29 *(28)*

[1] *A Psalm of David.*

Ascríbe to the Lórd, you héavenly pówers,
ascríbe to the Lórd glóry and stréngth.
[2] Ascríbe to the Lórd the glóry of God's náme;
bow dówn before the Lórd, majéstic in hóliness.

[3] The vóice of the Lórd upon the wáters,
the Gód of glóry thúnders;
the Lórd on the imménsity of wáters;
[4] the vóice of the Lórd full of pówer;
the vóice of the Lórd full of spléndor.

[5] The vóice of the Lórd shatters cédars,
the Lord shátters the cédars of Lébanon,
[6] making Lébanon léap like a cálf,
and Sírion like a yóung wild óx.

[7] The vóice of the Lórd flashes flámes of fíre.
[8] The vóice of the Lórd shakes the wílderness,
the Lord shákes the wílderness of Kádesh;
[9] the vóice of the Lórd rends the óak tree
and stríps the fórest báre.
In God's témple they áll cry, "Glóry!"

[10] The Lórd sits enthróned above the flóod;
the Lórd sits as kíng foréver.
[11] Give stréngth to your péople, O Lórd.
O Lórd, bless your péople with péace.

Psalm 30 (29)

[1] *A Psalm. A Canticle for the Dedication of the Temple. Of David.*

[2] I will extól you, Lórd, for you have ráised me úp,
and have nót let my énemies rejóice over mé.

[3] O Lord my Gód, I críed to you for hélp,
and yóu have héaled me.
[4] O Lórd, you have lífted up my sóul from Shéol,
restóred me to lífe from those who sínk into the pít.

[5] Sing psálms to the Lórd, you fáithful ones;
give thánks to God's hóly náme.
[6] Divine ánger lasts a móment, but fávor all through lífe.
At níght come téars, but dáwn brings jóy.

[7] I sáid to mysélf in my good fórtune:
"Í shall néver be sháken."
[8] O Lord, your fávor had sét me like a móuntain strónghold.
Then you híd your fáce, and I was pút to confúsion.

[9] To yóu, O Lórd, I críed,
to my Lórd I appéaled for mércy:
[10] "What prófit is my lífeblood, my góing to the grave?
Can dúst give you thánks, or procláim your fáithfulness?"

[11] Hear, O Lórd, and have mércy on mé;
bé my hélper, O Lórd.
[12] You have chánged my móurning into dáncing,
removed my sáckcloth and gírded me with jóy.
[13] So let my sóul sing psálms to you and nót be sílent.
O Lórd my Gód, I will thánk you forever.

Psalm 31 (30)

[1] *For the Choirmaster. A Psalm of David.*

[2] In yóu, O LÓRD, I take réfuge.
Let me néver be pút to sháme.
In your ríghteousness, sét me frée;
[3] incline your éar to me, and spéedily réscue me.

Be a róck of réfuge for mé,
a míghty strónghold to sáve me.
[4] For yóu are my róck, my strónghold!
Lead me, guíde me, for the sáke of your náme.

[5] Reléase me from the snáre they have hídden,
for yóu indéed are my réfuge.
[6] Into your hánds I comménd my spírit.
You will redéem me, O LÓRD, O faithful Gód.

[7] You detést those who sérve empty ídols.
As for mé, I trúst in the LÓRD.

[8] Let me be glád and rejóice in your lóve,
for yóu who have séen my afflíction
and taken héed of my sóul's distréss,
[9] have not léft me in the hánds of the énemy,
but sét my féet at lárge.

[10] Have mércy on mé, O Lórd,
for Í am in distréss.
My eyes are wásted awáy with gríef,
as are my sóul and my bódy.

[11] For my lífe is spént with sórrow,
and my yéars with síghs.
Afflíction has bróken down my stréngth,
and my bónes waste awáy.

[12] Becáuse of áll my fóes
I have becóme a repróach,
an óbject of scórn to my néighbors
and of féar to my fríends.

Those who sée me in the stréet, they flée from mé.
[13] I am forgótten, like sómeone déad,
and have becóme like a bróken véssel.

[14] I have héard the slánder of the crówd;
térror all aróund me,
as they plót togéther agáinst me,
as they plán to take my lífe.

[15] But as for mé, I trúst in you, O Lórd;
I say, "Yóu are my Gód.
[16] Thére in your hánds is my lót;
from the hánds of my énemies delíver me,
and from thóse who pursúe me.

[17] "Lét your face shíne on your sérvant.
Sáve me in your fáithful lóve.
[18] Let me nót be put to sháme, O Lórd,
for I cáll on yóu;
Lét the wícked be shámed!
Let them be sílenced in Shéol!

[19] "Let lýing líps be stílled,
that speak háughtily agáinst the ríghteous
with príde and contémpt."

[20] How gréat is the góodness, Lórd,
that you kéep for thóse who féar you,
that you shów to thóse who trúst you
in the síght of the chíldren of Ádam.

[21] You híde them in the shélter of your présence,
secúre from human schéming;
you kéep them sáfe within your tént
from dispúting tóngues.

[22] Blést be the Lórd who has wóndrously shówn me
faithful lóve in a fórtified cíty!

[23] "I am fár remóved from your síght,"
I sáid in my alárm.
Yet you héard the vóice of my pléa
when I críed to you for hélp.

[24] Lóve the Lórd, all you his sáints.
The Lórd guards the fáithful.
But the Lórd will repáy to the fúll
the one who ácts with príde.
[25] Be stróng, let your héart take cóurage,
all who hópe in the Lórd.

Psalm 32 *(31)*

[1] *Of David. A* Maskil.

Blessed is óne whose transgréssion is forgíven,
whose sín is remítted.
[2] Blessed the óne to whom the Lórd imputes no guílt,
in whose spírit is no guíle.

[3] I kept it sécret and my fráme was wásted.
I gróaned all day lóng,
[4] For your hánd, by dáy and by níght,
lay héavy upón me.
Indéed, my stréngth was dried úp
as by the súmmer's héat.

[5] To yóu I have acknówledged my sín;
my guílt I did not híde.
I sáid, "I will conféss my transgréssion to the Lórd."
And yóu have forgíven the guílt of my sín.

[6] So let each fáithful one práy to yóu
in the tíme of néed.
The flóods of wáter may reach hígh,
but such a óne they shall not réach.

[7] Yóu are a híding place for mé;
you kéep me sáfe from distréss;
you surróund me with críes of delíverance.

[8] Í will instrúct you and téach you
the wáy you should gó;
I will fíx my éyes upón you.

[9] Be not like hórse and múle, unintélligent,
needing brídle and bít,
or élse they will nót appróach you.

[10] Mány sórrows has the wícked,
but loving kíndness surróunds the one who trústs
in the Lórd.

[11] Rejóice in the Lórd, exult you ríghteous!
Ring out your jóy, all you úpright of héart!

Psalm 33 (32)

[1] Ring out your jóy to the LÓRD, O you ríghteous;
for práise is fítting from the úpright.
[2] Give thánks to the LÓRD upon the hárp;
with a tén-stringed lúte sing songs to Gód.
[3] O síng a sóng that is néw;
play skíllfully, with shóuts of jóy.

[4] For the wórd of the LÓRD is úpright,
and áll God's wórks to be trústed.
[5] The LÓRD loves jústice and ríght;
God's fáithful lóve fills the éarth.

[6] By the wórd of the LÓRD the héavens were máde,
by the bréath of God's móuth, all their hóst.
[7] As in a flásk, God collécts the wáves of the ócean,
and stóres up the dépths of the séa.

[8] Let áll the earth féar the LÓRD,
all who líve in the wórld show réverence.
[9] God spóke, and it cáme to bé;
commánded and it stóod in pláce.

[10] The LORD frústrates the desígns of the nátions,
and deféats the pláns of the péoples.
[11] The desígns of the LÓRD stand foréver,
the pláns of God's héart from age to áge.

[12] Blessed the nátion whose Gód is the LÓRD,
the péople God has chósen as a héritage.
[13] From the héavens the LÓRD looks fórth,
and sées the whóle human ráce.

[14] From the héavenly dwélling God gázes
on áll the dwéllers on the éarth,
[15] God who shápes the héarts of them áll,
and consíders áll their déeds.

[16] A rúler is not sáved by a great ármy,
nor a wárrior presérved by great stréngth.
[17] A vain hópe for sáfety is the hórse;
despite its pówer it cánnot sáve.

[18] Behóld, the éyes of the LÓRD
are on thóse who féar him,
who hópe in God's fáithful lóve,
[19] to réscue their sóul from déath,
to kéep them alíve in fámine.

[20] Our sóul is wáiting for the LÓRD,
our Gód, our hélp and our shíeld.
[21] In yóu do our héarts find jóy;
we trúst in your hóly náme.
[22] May your fáithful lóve be upón us,
as we hópe in yóu, O LÓRD.

Psalm 34 *(33)*

[1] *Of David, when he feigned madness before*
Abimelech, so that he drove him out,
and he went away.

[2] I will bléss the LÓRD at all tímes;
práise is álways in my móuth.
[3] In the LÓRD my sóul shall make its bóast;
the húmble shall héar and be glád.

[4] Glórify the LÓRD with mé;
togéther let us práise God's náme.
[5] I sóught the LÓRD, who ánswered me,
and sét me frée from all my térrors.

[6] Lóok towards the Lórd and be rádiant;
let your fáces nót be abáshed.
[7] When the lówly call óut, the LORD héars,
and réscues them from áll their distréss.

[8] The ángel of the LÓRD is encámped
around thóse who are réverent, to réscue them.
[9] Taste and sée that the LÓRD is góod.
Blessed are théy who seek réfuge in hím.

[10] Féar the LÓRD, you hóly ones.
They lack nóthing, thóse who fear Gód.
[11] The rích suffer wánt and go húngry,
but thóse who seek the LÓRD lack no bléssing.

[12] Cóme, chíldren, and héar me,
that I may téach you the féar of the LÓRD.
[13] Whó is éager for lífe
and lóngs to see prósperous dáys?

[14] Guárd your tóngue from évil,
and your líps from spéaking decéit.
[15] Turn asíde from évil and do góod.
Séek after péace, and pursúe it.

[16] The éyes of the LÓRD are on the ríghteous;
God's éars are ópen to their crý.
[17] The LORD's fáce is túrned against the wícked
to cut óff their remémbrance from the éarth.

[18] When the ríghteous cry óut, the LORD héars,
and réscues them in áll their distréss.
[19] The LORD is clóse to the brókenhéarted,
and sáves those whose spírit is crúshed.

[20] Mány are the tríals of the ríghteous,
but from them áll the LÓRD will réscue them,
[21] God keeps guárd over áll their bónes;
not óne of their bónes shall be brókеn.

[22] Évil brings déath to the wícked;
those who háte the ríghteous are dóomed.
[23] The sóuls of those who sérve the LORD are
ránsomed.
None who trúst in Gód shall be condémned.

***Psalm 35** (34)*

[1] *Of David.*

Conténd, O Lórd, with my conténders;
fíght those who fíght me.
[2] Táke up your búckler and shíeld;
aríse in my defénse.

[3] Táke up the jávelin and the spéar
against thóse who pursúe me.
Say to my sóul, "Í am your salvátion."

[4] Let thóse who séek my lífe
be shámed and disgráced.
Let thóse who plan évil agáinst me
be róuted in confúsion.

[5] Let them bé like cháff before the wínd;
let the ángel of the Lórd drive them ón.
[6] Let their páth be slíppery and dárk;
let the ángel of the Lórd pursúe them.

[7] Unprovóked, they have hídden a nét for me;
unprovóked, they have dúg a pít for me.
[8] Let rúin fáll upón them,
and táke them by surpríse.
Let them be cáught in the nét they have hídden;
let them fáll in their own pít.

[9] Then my sóul shall rejóice in the LÓRD,
and exúlt in God's salvátion.
[10] Áll my bónes will sáy,
"LORD, whó is like yóu
who réscue the wéak from the stróng
and the póor from the oppréssor?"

[11] Lýing wítnesses aríse,
asking me quéstions I cánnot understánd.
[12] They repáy me évil for góod;
my sóul is forlórn.

[13] When they were síck I dréssed in sáckcloth,
afflícted my sóul with fásting,
and with práyer ever néw in my héart,
[14] as for a bróther, a fríend.
I wént as though móurning a móther,
bowed dówn with gríef.

[15] Now that I stúmble, they gládly gáther;
they gáther, and móck me.
Í mysélf do not knów them,
yet strangers téar at me céaselessly.
[16] They provóke me with móckery on móckery,
and gnásh their teeth at mé.

[17] O LÓRD, how lóng will you look ón?
Réscue my lífe from their rávages,
my sóul from these líons.
[18] Then I will thánk you in the gréat assémbly;
amid the míghty thróng I will práise you.

[19] Do not lét my lýing fóes
rejóice over mé.
Do not lét those who háte me without cáuse
wink éyes at each óther.

[20] For théy do not spéak of péace,
but agáinst the quíet in the lánd
they concéive decéitful wórds,
[21] and, with móuths wide ópen,
they útter their crý agáinst me:
"Yes, yes! Our éyes have séen it!"

[22] O LÓRD, you have séen; do not be sílent;
Lórd, do not stánd far óff!
[23] Awáke! And stír to my defénse,
to my cáuse, O my Gód and my Lórd!

[24] Víndicate me, LÓRD, my Gód,
in accórd with your ríghteousness;
and lét them not rejóice over mé.

[25] Dó not let them thínk in their héarts,
"Yés, we have wón."
Dó not lét them sáy,
"Wé have destróyed you!"

[26] Let them be shámed and bróught to disgráce
who rejóice at my misfórtune.
Let them be cóvered with sháme and confúsion
who ráise themselves agáinst me.

[27] Lét them exúlt and be glád
who delíght in my delíverance.
Lét them sáy without énd,
"Gréat is the Lórd who delíghts
in the péace of this sérvant."

[28] Then my tóngue shall spéak of your ríghteousness,
and all day lóng of your práise.

Psalm 36 *(35)*

[1] *For the Choirmaster. Of David, the servant of the Lord.*

[2] Transgréssion spéaks to sínners
in the dépths of their héarts.
There is no féar of Gód before their éyes.

[3] In their own éyes, they flátter themsélves;
they do not sée and detést their own guílt.
[4] The wórds of their móuths are míschief and deceít.
They have céased to be prúdent and do góod.

[5] On their béds they plót iníquity.
They set their féet on évery wicked wáy;
no évil do théy rejéct.

[6] Your faithful lóve, O Lord, réaches to héaven,
your trúth to the clóuds.
[7] Your ríghteousness is líke the móuntains of Gód;
like the great déep, your jústice.
Both human béing and béast you sáve, O Lórd.

[8] How précious is your lóve, O Gód!
The chíldren of Ádam seek shélter
in the shádow óf your wíngs.

[9] They féast on the ríches of your hóuse;
you give them drínk from the stréam of your
delíght.
[10] For with yóu is the fóuntain of lífe,
and ín your líght we see líght.

[11] Maintain your lóve for thóse who knów you,
your saving jústice to úpright héarts.
[12] Let the fóot of the próud not tréad on me
nor the hánd of the wícked drive me óut.
[13] Thére have the évildoers fállen;
flung dówn, unáble to ríse!

Psalm 37 (36)

[1] *Of David.*

Do not frét becáuse of the wícked;
do not énvy thóse who do évil,
[2] for they wíther quíckly like gráss
and fáde like the gréen of the fíelds.

[3] Trúst in the LÓRD and do góod;
then you will dwéll in the lánd and find safe
    pásture.
[4] Fínd your delíght in the LÓRD,
who gránts your héart's desíre.

[5] Commít your wáy to the LÓRD;
if you trúst, then Gód will áct,
[6] and make your ríghteousness shíne like the líght,
your jústice like the nóonday sún.

[7] Be stíll before the LÓRD and wait in pátience;
do not frét at the óne who próspers,
the óne who makes évil plóts.

[8] Calm your ánger and forgét your ráge;
do not frét, it ónly leads to évil.
[9] For thóse who do évil shall pérish.
But thóse who hópe in the LÓRD,
théy shall inhérit the lánd.

[10] A little lónger–and the wícked are góne.
Lóok at their pláce: they are not thére.
[11] But the méek shall inhérit the lánd
and delíght in fúllness of péace.

[12] The wícked plót against the ríghteous
and gnásh their téeth agáinst them;
[13] but the Lórd will láugh at the wícked,
séeing that their dáy is at hánd.

[14] The wícked draw the swórd, bend their bóws,
to sláughter the póor and néedy,
to sláy those whose wáys are úpright.
[15] Their swórd shall píerce their own héarts,
and their bóws shall be bróken to píeces.

[16] How much bétter the líttle of the ríghteous,
than the óverflowing wéalth of the wícked;
[17] for the árms of the wícked shall be bróken,
and the Lórd will suppórt the ríghteous.

[18] The Lord takes nóte of the dáys of the blámeless;
their héritage will lást foréver.
[19] They shall nót be put to sháme in evil dáys;
in time of fámine they shall háve their fíll.

[20] But áll the wícked shall pérish;
the énemies of the Lórd shall be consúmed.
Théy are like the béauty of the méadows;
they shall vánish, they shall vánish like smóke.

[21] The wicked bórrows and does nót repáy,
but the ríghteous is génerous and gíves.
[22] Those blessed by Gód shall inhérit the lánd,
while thóse who are cúrsed shall be cut óff.

[23] By the LÓRD are the stéps of a wárrior
made fírm in delíght of God's wáys.
[24] Though they stúmble they shall néver fáll,
for the LÓRD will hóld them by the hánd.

[25] I was yóung and nów I am óld,
but I have néver seen the ríghteous forsáken
nor their chíldren bégging for bréad.
[26] All the dáy they are génerous and lénd,
and their chíldren becóme a bléssing.

[27] Then túrn away from évil and do góod,
and yóu may abíde forever;
[28] for indéed, the LÓRD loves jústice,
and will néver forsáke the fáithful.

The unjúst shall be wíped out forever,
and the descéndants of the wícked cut óff.
[29] The ríghteous shall inhérit the lánd;
thére they shall abíde forever.

[30] The móuths of the ríghteous utter wísdom,
and their tóngues tell fórth what is júst.
[31] The láw of Gód is in their héarts;
their stéps shall be sáved from stúmbling.

[32] The wícked keep wátch for the ríghteous,
and séek an occásion to destróy them.
[33] The Lórd will not léave them in their pówer,
nor lét them be condémned when they are
júdged.

[34] Then wáit for the Lórd, keep to the wáy.
God will exált you to inhérit the lánd,
and you will sée the wícked cut óff.

[35] I have séen the wícked triúmphant,
tówering like cédars of Lébanon.
[36] I pássed by agáin; they were góne.
I séarched; they were nówhere to be fóund.

[37] Mark the blámeless, obsérve the úpright;
for the péaceful a fúture lies in stóre,
[38] but sínners shall áll be destróyed,
the fúture of the wícked cut óff.

[39] But from the Lórd comes the salvátion of the
ríghteous,
their strónghold in tíme of distréss.
[40] The Lord hélps them and réscues thém,
réscues and sáves them from the wícked,
for their réfuge is in Gód.

Psalm 38 (*37*)

[1] *A Psalm of David. For a Memorial.*

[2] O Lórd, do not rebúke me in your ánger;
reprôve me nót in your ráge.
[3] For your árrows have sunk déep in mé;
your hánd has come dówn upón me.

[4] There is no sóundness in my flésh becáuse of your ánger:
There is no héalth in my bónes becáuse of my sín.

[5] My guílt towers hígher than my héad;
it is a wéight too héavy to béar.
[6] My wóunds are fóul and féstering,
the resúlt of mý own fólly.
[7] I am bówed and bróught to my knées.
I go móurning áll the day lóng.

[8] All my fráme is búrning with féver;
thére is no sóundness in my flésh.
[9] I am spént and útterly crúshed,
I cry alóud in ánguish of héart.

[10] O Lórd, all my lónging lies befóre you;
my gróans are not hídden from yóu.
[11] My heart thróbs, my stréngth is spént;
the very líght has góne from my éyes.

[12] Friends and compánions stand alóof from my
íllness;
those clósest to me stánd far óff.
[13] Those who plót against my lífe lay snáres;
those who séek my rúin speak of hárm,
planning tréachery áll the day lóng.

[14] But Í, like someone déaf, do not héar;
like someone múte, I do not ópen my móuth.
[15] Í am like óne who hears nóthing,
in whose móuth is nó defénse.

[16] But for yóu, O Lórd, I wáit;
it is yóu, Lord my Gód, who will ánswer.
[17] I pray, "Lét them not glóat over mé,
exúlt if my fóot should slíp."

[18] For Í am on the póint of fálling,
and my páin is álways wíth me.
[19] I conféss that Í am guílty;
and I am gríeved becáuse of my sín.

[20] My énemies live ón and grow stróng,
and mány háte me without cáuse.
[21] They repáy me évil for góod,
and attáck me for séeking what is góod.

[22] Forsáke me nót, O Lórd!
My Gód, be not fár from mé!
[23] Make háste and cóme to my hélp,
my Lórd and mý salvátion!

Psalm 39 *(38)*

[1] *For the Choirmaster, for Jeduthun. A Psalm of David.*

[2] I sáid, "I will be wátchful of my wáys,
for féar I should sín with my tóngue.
I will pút a cúrb on my líps
when the wícked stánd befóre me."
[3] I was múte, sílent, very stíll,
as my páin becáme inténse.

[4] My héart was búrning withín me.
With these thóughts, the fíre blazed úp,
and my tóngue burst fórth into spéech:
[5] "O Lórd, you have shówn me my énd,
how shórt is the léngth of my dáys.
Now I knów how fléeting is my lífe.

[6] "How shórt the span of dáys you have gíven me;
my lífe is as nóthing in your síght.
Surely áll people stánd as but a bréath.
[7] Surely éach of us líves as a shádow,
surely stored ríches áre as a mere bréath;
we dó not knów who will gáther them."

[8] And nów, Lord, whát is there to wáit for?
In yóu rests áll my hópe.
[9] Set me frée from áll my síns,
do not máke me the táunt of the fóol.
[10] I was sílent, not ópening my líps,
because thís was áll your dóing.

[11] Take awáy your scóurge from mé.
I am crúshed by the blóws of your hánd.
[12] You chastíse us, sínners, with due púnishment;
like a móth you devóur all we tréasure.
We are áll of us no móre than a bréath.

[13] O Lórd, give héed to my práyer;
túrn your éar to my crý;
dó not be déaf to my wéeping.
Behóld, I am a stránger to yóu,
a pílgrim, like áll my fórebears.

[14] Look awáy from me that Í may smíle
befóre I depárt to be no móre.

Psalm 40 *(39)*

[1] *For the Choirmaster. Of David. A Psalm.*

[2] I wáited, I wáited for the Lórd,
and God stóoped down to mé,
having héard my crý.

[3] The Lord dréw me from the déadly pít,
from the míry cláy.
God sét my féet upon a róck,
made my fóotsteps fírm.

[4] The Lord pút a new sóng into my móuth,
práise of our Gód.
Mány shall sée and féar
and shall trúst in the Lórd.

[5] Bléssed are théy who have pláced
their trúst in the Lórd,
and dó not túrn to the próud
who fóllow false góds.

[6] How mány are the wónders and desígns
that you have wórked for us, O Lórd my Gód;
you háve no équal.
Should I wísh to procláim or spéak of them,
they would be móre than I can téll!

[7] You delíght not in sácrifice and óffering,
but in an ópen éar.
You do not ásk for hólocaust and sín offering.

[8] Then I sáid, "Behóld, I have cóme."
In the scróll of the bóok it stands wrítten of mé:
[9] "I delíght to do your wíll, O my Gód;
your instrúction lies déep withín me."

[10] Your ríghteousness I háve procláimed
in the gréat assémbly.
My líps I háve not séaled;
you knów it, O Lórd.

[11] Your saving hélp I have not hídden in my héart;
of your fáithful salvátion I have spóken.
I made no sécret of your grácious lóve
and your trúth to the gréat assémbly.

[12] You, O Lórd, will not withhóld your
compássion from mé.
Your loving kíndness and your fáithfulness will
álways guárd me.

[13] For Í am besét with évils
too mány to be cóunted.
My iníquities have óvertáken me,
till I can sée no móre.
They are móre than the háirs of my héad,
and my héart is sínking.

[14] Be pléased, O Lórd, to réscue me;
Lord, make háste to hélp me.
[15] O lét there be sháme and confúsion
on those who séek my lífe.

O lét them turn báck in confúsion
who delíght in my hárm.
[16] Let them be appálled becáuse of their sháme,
those who jéer and móck me.

[17] O lét there be rejóicing and gládness
for áll who séek you.
Let them éver say, "The Lórd is gréat,"
who lóng for your salvátion.

[18] Wrétched and póor though I ám,
the Lord is míndful of mé.
Yóu are my réscuer, my hélp;
O my Gód, do not deláy.

Psalm 41 *(40)*

[1] *For the Choirmaster. A Psalm of David.*

[2] Blessed are théy who have concérn for the póor.
In time of tróuble, the Lórd will réscue them.

[3] The Lord will guárd them, presérve their lífe,
and máke them bléssed in the lánd,
not give them úp to the wíll of their fóes.

[4] The LORD will hélp them on their béd of páin;
in their síckness, you tend éven to their bédding.

[5] As for mé, I said, "LÓRD, have mércy on mé;
héal my sóul, for I have sínned agáinst you."
[6] My fóes speak évil agáinst me and wónder,
how lóng before I díe and my náme is forgótten?
[7] When they cóme to vísit me, they spéak empty
wórds.
Their héarts store up málice; on léaving, they
spread líes.

[8] All my foes whísper togéther agáinst me.
They devíse evil plóts agáinst me,
[9] Saying sómething déadly has fástened upón me,
that I wíll not ríse from where I líe.

[10] Thus éven my fríend, in whom I trústed,
who áte my bréad,
has lífted a héel agáinst me.

[11] But yóu, O LÓRD, have mércy on mé.
Raise me úp and Í will repáy them.
[12] By thís I knów your fávor:
that my fóes do not tríumph over mé.
[13] In my intégrity yóu have uphéld me,
and have sét me in your présence foréver.

* * *

[14] Blést be the LÓRD, the Gód of Ísrael,
from áge to áge. Amén. Amén.

BOOK TWO OF THE PSALTER

Psalm 42 *(41)*

[1] *For the Choirmaster. A* Maskil. *Of the sons of Korah.*

[2] Like the déer that yéarns for running stréams,
so my sóul is yéarning for yóu, my Gód.

[3] My soul is thírsting for Gód, the living Gód;
when can I énter and appéar before the fáce of Gód?

[4] My téars have becóme my bréad,
by dáy, by níght,
as they sáy to me áll the day lóng,
"Whére is your Gód?"

[5] These thíngs will I remémber as I póur out my sóul:
for I would gó to the pláce of your wóndrous tént,
all the wáy to the hóuse of Gód,
amid críes of gládness and thanksgíving,
the thróng keeping jóyful féstival.

[6] Whý are you cast dówn, my sóul;
why gróan withín me?
Hope in Gód, whom I will práise yet agáin,
my saving présence and my Gód.

[7] My sóul is cast dówn withín me,
thérefore I remémber you
from the lánd of Jórdan and Mount Hérmon,
from the Híll of Mízar.

[8] Déep is cálling on déep,
in the róar of your tórrents;
your bíllows and áll your wáves
swépt over mé.

[9] By dáy the Lord decrées loving mércy;
by níght a sóng is with mé,
a práyer to the Gód of my lífe.

[10] I will sáy to Gód, my róck,
"Whý have you forgótten me?
Whý do Í go móurning
oppréssed by the fóe?"

[11] With a déadly wóund in my bónes,
my énemies revíle me,
sáying to me áll the day lóng,
"Whére is your Gód?"

[12] Whý are you cast dówn, my sóul;
why gróan withín me?
Hope in Gód, whom I will práise yet agáin,
my saving présence and my Gód.

Psalm 43 *(42)*

[1] Give me jústice, O Gód, and plead my cáuse
against a nátion that is fáithless.
From thóse who are decéitful and cúnning
réscue me, O Gód.

[2] Yóu, O Gód, are my stréngth;
whý have you rejécted me?
Whý do Í go móurning,
opprésséd by the fóe?

[3] O sénd forth your líght and your trúth;
they will guíde me ón.
They will bríng me to your hóly móuntain,
to the pláce where you dwéll.

[4] And I will cóme to the áltar of Gód,
to God, my jóy and gládness.
To yóu will I give thánks on the hárp,
O Gód, my Gód.

[5] Whý are you cast dówn, my sóul;
why gróan withín me?
Hope in Gód, whom I will práise yet agáin,
my saving présence and my Gód.

Psalm 44 *(43)*

[1] *For the Choirmaster. Of the sons of Korah.*
A Maskil.

[2] We héard with our own éars, O Gód;
our fórebears have decláred to ús
the déeds you díd in their dáys,
you yoursélf, in dáys long agó.

[3] With your own hánd you dróve out the nátions,
but thém you plánted;
You brought afflíction on the péoples;
but thém you set frée.

[4] No swórd of their ówn won the lánd;
no árm of their ówn brought them víctory.
It was yóur right hánd and your árm,
and the líght of your fáce, for you lóved them.

[5] Yóu are my rúler, O Gód;
you cómmand the víctories for Jácob.
[6] Through yóu we béat down our fóes;
in your náme we trámpled our aggréssors.

[7] For it was nót in my bów that I trústed,
nor yét was I sáved by my swórd:
[8] it was yóu who sáved us from our fóes;
those who háte us, you pút to sháme.
[9] All day lóng our bóast was in Gód,
and we will práise your náme foréver.

[10] Yet nów you have rejécted us, disgráced us;
you no lónger go fórth with our ármies.
[11] You máke us retréat from the fóe;
those who háte us plúnder us at wíll.

[12] You máke us like shéep for the sláughter,
and scátter us amóng the nátions.
[13] You séll your own péople for nóthing,
and máke no prófit by the sále.

[14] You máke us the táunt of our néighbors,
the móckery and scórn of those aróund us.
[15] Among the nátions you máke us a býword;
among the péoples they sháke their héads.

[16] All day lóng my disgráce is befóre me;
my fáce is cóvered with sháme
[17] at the vóice of the táunter, the scóffer,
at the síght of the fóe and avénger.

[18] This beféll us though wé had not forgótten you;
wé were not fálse to your cóvenant.
[19] We had nót withdráwn our héarts;
our féet had not stráyed from your páth.
[20] Yet you have crúshed us in a háunt of jáckals,
and overwhélmed us with the shádow of déath.

[21] Had we forgótten the náme of our Gód,
or strétched out our hánds to a strange gód,
[22] would not Gód have fóund this óut,
who knóws the sécrets of the héart?
[23] It is for yóu we are sláin all day lóng,
and are cóunted as shéep for the sláughter.

[24] Awáke, O Lord! Whý do you sléep?
Aríse! Do not rejéct us foréver.
[25] Whý do you híde your fáce,
and forgét our oppréssion and mísery?

[26] For our sóul is brought lów to the dúst;
our bódy lies próstrate on the éarth.
[27] Stand úp and cóme to our hélp!
Redéem us with your mérciful lóve!

Psalm 45 *(44)*

[1] *For the Choirmaster. Intoned like "The Lilies."*
Of the sons of Korah. A Maskil. *A Love Song.*

[2] My héart overflóws with nóble wórds.
To the kíng I addréss the sóng I have máde,
my tóngue as nímble as the pén of a scríbe.

[3] Yóu are the most hándsome of the sóns of mén,
and gráciousness is póured out upón your líps,
for Gód has bléssed you forévermóre.

[4] Gírd your swórd upon your thígh, O míghty one,
with your spléndor and your májesty.
[5] In your májesty ríde on in tríumph
for the cáuse of fáithfulness and clémency and
righteousness.
May your ríght hand shów your wóndrous déeds.

[6] Your árrows are shárp
in the héart of the fóes of the kíng.
Péoples fáll benéath you.

[7] Your thróne, O Gód, shall endúre forév er.
A scépter of jústice is the scépter of your kíngdom.
[8] Your lóve is for ríghteousness; your hátred for évil.

Thérefore Gód, your Gód, has anóinted you
with the óil of gládness abóve your compánions:
[9] all your róbes are frágrant with áloes, myrrh, and
cássia.

From the ívory pálace you are gláddened with
músic.
[10] The dáughters of kíngs are thóse whom you fávor.
At your ríght stands the quéen in góld of Óphir.

[11] Lísten, O dáughter; pay héed and give éar:
forgét your own péople and your fáther's hóuse.
[12] Só will the kíng desíre your béauty.
Hé is your lórd, pay hómage to hím.
[13] And the dáughter of Týre shall cóme with gífts;
the ríchest of the péople shall séek your fávor.

[14] The dáughter of the kíng is clóthed with
splendor;
her róbes are thréaded with góld.
[15] In fine clóthing shé is léd to the kíng;
behínd her, her máiden compánions fóllow.
[16] Théy are escórted amid gládness and jóy;
they páss withín the pálace of the kíng.

[17] Sóns will be yóurs to succéed your fáthers;
you will máke them rúlers over áll the éarth.
[18] I will máke your náme forever remémbered.
Thus the péoples will práise you from áge to áge.

Psalm 46 (45)

[1] *For the Choirmaster. Of the sons of Korah. Intoned like "The Maidens." A Song.*

[2] Gód is for ús a réfuge and stréngth,
an éver-present hélp in tíme of distréss:
[3] so wé shall not féar though the éarth should róck,
though the móuntains quáke to the héart of the séa;
[4] éven though its wáters ráge and fóam,
éven though the móuntains be sháken by its túmult.

The Lórd of hósts is wíth us:
the Gód of Jácob is our strónghold.

[5] The wáters of a ríver give jóy to God's cíty,
the holy pláce, the abóde of the Most Hígh.
[6] Gód is withín her, she cánnot be sháken;
Gód will hélp her at the dáwning of the dáy.
[7] Nátions are in túmult, kíngdoms are sháken:
a divíne voice róars, and the éarth melts awáy.

[8] The Lórd of hósts is wíth us:
the Gód of Jácob is our strónghold.

[9] Cóme and behóld the wórks of the Lórd,
the áwesome déeds God has dóne on the éarth.
[10] God puts an énd to wárs over áll the éarth;
breaking bóws, snapping spéars, and burning
shíelds with fíre:
[11] "Be stíll and knów that Í am Gód,
exálted over nátions, exálted over éarth!"

[12] The Lórd of hósts is wíth us:
the Gód of Jácob is our strónghold.

Psalm 47 *(46)*

[1] *For the Choirmaster. Of the sons of Korah. A Psalm.*

[2] All péoples, cláp your hánds.
Cry to Gód with shóuts of jóy!
[3] For the Lórd, the Most Hígh, is áwesome,
the great kíng over áll the éarth.

[4] God húmbles péoples under ús
and nátions únder our féet.
[5] Our héritage God chóse for ús,
the príde of Jácob the belóved.

[6] God has gone úp with shóuts of jóy.
The Lord goes úp with trúmpet blást.
[7] Sing práise for Gód; sing práise!
Sing práise to our kíng; sing práise!
[8] For God is kíng of áll the éarth.
Sing práise with a hýmn.

[9] Gód is réigning over nátions,
God síts upon a hóly thróne.
[10] The léaders of the péoples are assémbled
with the péople of the Gód of Ábraham.
For the rúlers of the éarth belong to Gód,
whó is gréatly exálted.

Psalm 48 *(47)*

[1] *A Song. A Psalm. Of the sons of Korah.*

[2] Great is the LÓRD and híghly to be práised
in the cíty of our Gód,
[3] whose holy móuntain ríses in béauty,
the jóy of all the éarth.

Mount Zíon, in the héart of the Nórth,
the cíty of the Míghty Kíng!
[4] Gód, in the mídst of her cítadels,
is shówn to bé her strónghold.

[5] Behóld! the kíngs assémbled;
togéther they advánced.
[6] They sáw; at ónce they márveled;
dismáyed, they fled in féar.

[7] A trémbling séized them thére,
anguish, like pángs in giving bírth,
[8] As whén the éast wind shátters
the shíps of Társhish.

[9] As wé have héard, so we have séen
in the cíty of our Gód,
in the cíty of the LÓRD of hósts,
which God estáblishes forévér.

[10] Your fáithful lóve, O Gód,
we pónder in your témple.
[11] Your práise, O Gód, like your náme,
reaches the énds of the éarth.

Your right hánd is fílled with saving jústice.
[12] Mount Zíon rejóices.
The dáughters of Júdah rejóice
at the síght of your júdgments.

[13] Walk through Zíon, wálk all aróund her;
count the númber of her tówers.
[14] Consíder áll her rámparts;
exámine her cástles,

That you may téll the néxt generátion
[15] that súch is our Gód,
Our Gód foréver and álways,
who will guíde us foréver.

Psalm 49 *(48)*

[1] *For the Choirmaster. Of the sons of Korah. A Psalm.*

[2] Héar this, áll you péoples,
give éar, all who dwéll in the wórld,
[3] péople both hígh and lów,
rích and póor alíke!

[4] My móuth will útter wísdom.
The refléctions of my héart offer ínsight.
[5] I will inclíne my éar to a mýstery;
with the hárp I will sét forth my próblem.

[6] Whý should I féar in evil dáys
the málice of the fóes who surróund me,
[7] thóse who trúst in their wéalth,
and bóast of the vástness of their ríches?

[8] No one can ránsom a bróther or a síster,
nor pay a príce to Gód for a lífe.
[9] How hígh is the príce of a sóul!
The ránsom can néver be enóugh!
[10] Nó one can búy life unénding,
nor avóid going dówn to the pít.

[11] We sée that the wíse will díe;
the fóolish will pérish with the sénseless,
and léave their wéalth to óthers.

[12] Their gráves are their hómes foréver,
their dwélling place from áge to áge,
though lánds were cálled by their námes.

[13] In their ríches, human béings do nót endúre;
théy are like the béasts that pérish.

[14] Thís is the wáy of the fóolish,
the óutcome of those pléased with their lót:
[15] like shéep they are dríven to Shéol,
where déath shall becóme their shépherd,
and the úpright shall háve domínion.

Their outward shów wastes awáy with the mórning,
and Shéol becómes their hóme.
[16] But God will ránsom my sóul from the grásp of
Shéol;
for Gód indéed will recéive me.

[17] Then do not féar when péople grow rích,
when the glóry of their hóuses incréases.
[18] They take nóthing wíth them when they díe,
their glóry does not fóllow them belów.

[19] Though they fláttered themsélves while they líved,
"People will práise you for áll your succéss,"
[20] yet you will gó to jóin your fórebears,
and will néver see the líght anymóre.

[21] In their ríches, human béings cannót discérn;
théy are like the béasts that pérish.

Psalm 50 *(49)*

[1] *A Psalm* of *Asaph.*

The Gód of góds, the Lórd,
has spóken and súmmoned the éarth,
from the rísing of the sún to its sétting.
[2] Out of Zíon, the perféction of béauty,
Gód is shíning fórth.

[3] Our God cómes, and does nót keep sílence.
In advánce, a fíre devóurs,
all aróund, a témpest ráges,
[4] God súmmons the héavens abóve
and the éarth, to júdge the péople.

[5] "Gáther my fáithful ones to mé,
who made cóvenant with mé by sácrifice."
[6] The héavens procláim divine ríghteousness,
for Gód, indéed, is the júdge.

[7] "Lísten, my péople, I will spéak;
Ísrael, I will téstify agáinst you,
for Í am Gód, your Gód.

[8] "I do nót rebúke you for your sácrifices;
your ófferings are álways befóre me.
[9] I do not táke more búllocks from your fárms,
nor góats from amóng your hérds.

[10] "For I ówn all the béasts of the fórest,
béasts in their thóusands on my hílls.
[11] I knów all the bírds on the móuntains;
all that móves in the fíeld belongs to mé.

[12] "Were I húngry, Í would not téll you,
for the wórld and its fúllness is míne.
[13] Do I éat the flésh of búlls,
or drínk the blóod of góats?

[14] "Give your práise as a sácrifice to Gód,
and fulfíll your vóws to the Most Hígh.
[15] Then call on mé in the dáy of distréss.
I will delíver you and yóu shall hónor me."

[16] But Gód will sáy to the wícked,
"Hów can you recíte my commándments,
and take my cóvenant ón your líps,
[17] yóu who despíse corréction,
and cást my wórds behínd you,

[18] "Yóu who see thíeves and befríend them,
who thrów in your lót with adúlterers,
[19] who unbrídle your móuth for évil,
and yóke your tóngue to decéit,

[20] "You who sít and malígn your own kín,
and slánder your own bróthers and sísters?
[21] You do thís, and should Í keep sílence?
Do you thínk that Í am like yóu?
I accúse you, lay the chárge befóre you.

[22] "Mark this, yóu who are forgétful of Gód,
lest I séize you and nó one can delíver you.
[23] A sácrifice of práise gives me hónor,
and to óne whose wáy is blámeless,
I will shów the salvátion of Gód."

Psalm 51 *(50)*

[1] *For the Choirmaster. A Psalm of David* [2] *when the prophet Nathan came to him after he had gone to Bathsheba.*

[3] Have mércy on mé, O Gód,
accórding to your mérciful lóve;
accórding to your gréat compássion,
blót out mý transgréssions.
[4] O wásh me complétely from my guílt,
and cléanse me fróm my sín.

[5] My transgréssions, trúly I knów them;
my sín is álways befóre me.
[6] Against yóu, you alóne, have I sínned;
what is évil in your síght I have dóne.
So yóu are júst in your séntence,
withóut repróach in your júdgment.

[7] Behóld, in guílt I was bórn,
a sínner when my móther concéived me.
[8] Behóld, you delíght in sincérity of héart;
in sécret you téach me wísdom.
[9] Cleanse me with hýssop, and Í shall be púre;
wash me, and Í shall be whíter than snów.

[10] Let me héar rejóicing and gládness,
that the bónes you have crúshed may exúlt.
[11] Túrn away your fáce from my síns,
and blót out áll my guílt.

[12] Creáte a pure héart for me, O Gód;
renew a stéadfast spírit withín me.
[13] Do not cást me awáy from your présence;
take not your hóly spírit from mé.

[14] Restóre in me the jóy of your salvátion;
sustáin in me a wílling spírit.
[15] I will téach transgréssors your wáys,
that sínners may retúrn to yóu.

[16] Réscue me from blóodshed, O Gód,
O Gód of mý salvátion,
and then my tóngue shall ring óut your
ríghteousness.
[17] O Lórd, ópen my líps
and my móuth shall procláim your práise.

[18] For in sácrifice you táke no delíght;
burnt óffering from mé would not pléase you.
[19] My sácrifice to Gód, a broken spírit:
a bróken and húmbled héart,
you wíll not spúrn, O Gód.

[20] In your good pléasure, show fávor to Zíon;
rebuíld the wálls of Jerúsalem.
[21] Thén you will delíght in righteous sácrifice,
burnt ófferings whólly consúmed.
Thén you will be óffered young búlls on your
áltar.

Psalm 52 (51)

[1] *For the Choirmaster. A* Maskil *of David* [2] *after Doeg the Edomite came and told Saul, "David has gone to the house of Abimelech."*

[3] Whý do you bóast of wíckedness,
you chámpion of évil?
[4] Planning rúin áll day lóng,
your tóngue is like a shárpened rázor,
you who práctice decéit!

[5] You love évil móre than góod,
fálsehood more than trúth.
[6] You love évery destrúctive wórd,
O tóngue of decéit.

[7] Then God will bréak you dówn foréver,
and will táke you awáy,
Will snátch you from your tént, and upróot you
from the lánd of the líving.

[8] The ríghteous shall sée and féar.
They shall láugh and sáy,
[9] "Behóld the chámpion who refúsed
to take Gód as a strónghold,
but trústed in the gréatness of wéalth
and grew pówerful by wíckedness."

[10] But Í am like a grówing ólive tree
in the hóuse of Gód.
I trúst in the fáithful lóve of Gód,
foréver and éver.

[11] I will thánk you forévermóre,
for thís is your dóing.
I will hópe in your náme, for it is góod,
in the présence of your fáithful.

Psalm 53 *(52)*

[1] *For the Choirmaster. Intoned like* Mahalat.
A Maskil *of David.*

[2] Fóols have sáid in their héarts,
"There ís no Gód."
Their déeds are corrúpt, depráved;
no one dóes any góod.

[3] Gód looks dówn from héaven
on the húman ráce,
to sée if ány are wíse,
if ány seek Gód.

[4] Áll have léft the right páth,
depráved, every óne;
there is nó one who dóes any góod,
nó, not even óne.

[5] Do nóne who do évil understánd?
They eat úp my péople as if éating bréad;
they néver call óut to Gód.

[6] Thére they shall trémble with féar –
without cáuse for féar –
for God scátters the bónes of your besiégers.
They are shámed; God rejécts them.

[7] Whó will bring Ísrael salvátion from Zíon?
When Gód brings abóut the retúrn of the péople,
then Jácob will be glád and Ísrael rejóice.

Psalm 54 *(53)*

[1] *For the Choirmaster. On stringed instruments. A* Maskil *of David* [2] *after the Ziphites came to Saul and said, "Is not David hiding among us?"*

[3] Sáve me, O Gód, by your náme;
by your pówer, defénd my cáuse.
[4] Héar my práyer, O Gód;
give éar to the wórds of my móuth.

[5] For strángers have rísen agáinst me,
and the rúthless séek my lífe.
They have nó regárd for Gód.

[6] Behóld, I have Gód for my hélp.
The Lórd sustáins my sóul.
[7] Let évil recóil on my fóes.
In your fáithfulness, bríng them to an énd.

[8] I will sácrifice to yóu with willing héart,
and praise your náme, O Lórd, for it is góod:
[9] for it has réscued me from áll distréss,
and my éyes have gázed upon my fóes.

Psalm 55 *(54)*

[1] *For the Choirmaster. On stringed instruments.*
A Maskil *of David.*

[2] Give éar, O Gód, to my práyer;
do not híde from my pléading.
[3] Atténd to mé and replý;
with my cáres, I cannot rést.

[4] I trémble at the shóuts of the fóe,
at the críes of the wícked,
for they píle up évil upón me;
in ánger they malígn me.

[5] My héart is strícken withín me;
death's térror falls upón me.
[6] Trémbling and féar come óver me,
and hórror overwhélms me.

[7] I say, "Ó that I had wíngs like a dóve,
to fly awáy and be at rést!
[8] I would indéed escápe far awáy,
and take réfuge in the désert.
[9] I would hásten to fínd my shélter
from the ráging wind and témpest."

[10] Confóund and confúse their tongues, O Lórd,
for I see víolence and strífe in the cíty!
[11] Night and dáy they patról its wálls.
In its mídst are wíckedness and évil.

[12] Destrúction líes withín it.
Its stréets are néver frée
from týranny and decéit.

[13] If an énemy made táunts agáinst me,
Í could béar it.
If my ríval had rísen agáinst me,
I could híde from such a óne.

[14] But it is yóu, as my équal, my fríend,
whom I knéw so wéll,
[15] with whóm I enjóyed friendly cóunsel!
We wálked togéther in hármony
in the hóuse of Gód.

[16] May déath fall súddenly upón them!
Let them go dówn alive to Shéol,
for wíckedness dwélls in their hómes,
and déep in their héarts.

[17] As for mé, I will crý to Gód,
and the Lórd will sáve me.
[18] Évening, mórning, and at nóon,
I will crý and lamént,
and God will héar my vóice.

[19] God will redéem my sóul in péace
in the attáck agáinst me,
for thóse who fíght me are mány.

[20] Gód, who is enthróned foréver,
will héar them and húmble them.
For théy will not aménd their wáys;
they have no féar of Gód.

[21] My fríend has túrned agáinst me,
has bróken our páct,
[22] with spéech that is sófter than bútter,
but with a héart set on wár;
with wórds that are smóother than óil,
but they are swórds unshéathed.

[23] Entrúst your cáres to the Lórd,
to Gód who will suppórt you,
who will néver allów the ríghteous to stúmble.

[24] But you will bríng them dówn, O Gód,
to the pít of déath:
thóse who are decéitful and blóodthirsty
shall not líve even hálf their dáys.
But Í, I will trúst in you, O Lórd.

Psalm 56 *(55)*

[1] *For the Choirmaster. Intoned like "The Dove of Distant Places." A* Miktam *of David, when the Philistines seized him in Gath.*

[2] Have mércy on mé, O Gód,
for péople assáil me;
they fíght me all day lóng and oppréss me.
[3] My fóes assáil me all day lóng:
mány fight próudly agáinst me.

[4] On the dáy when Í shall féar,
I will trúst in yóu,
[5] in Gód, whose wórd I práise.
In Gód I trúst; I shall not féar.
Whát can mere flésh do to mé?

[6] All day lóng they distórt my wórds,
their évery thought agáinst me is évil.
[7] They bánd togéther in ámbush;
they wátch my véry fóotsteps,
as they wáit to táke my lífe.

[8] Repáy them, O Gód, for their crímes;
in your ánger, bríng down the péoples.
[9] You have képt an accóunt of my wánderings;
you have pláced my téars in your flásk;
áre they not recórded in your bóok?

[10] Thén my fóes will turn báck
on the dáy when I cáll to yóu.

This I knów, that Gód is on my síde.
[11] In Gód, whose wórd I práise,
in the Lórd whose wórd I práise,
[12] in Gód I trúst; I shall not féar.
Whát can mere flésh do to mé?

[13] I am bóund by the vóws I have máde you.
O Gód, I will óffer you práise,
[14] for you have réscued my sóul from déath;
you képt my féet from stúmbling,
that I may wálk in the présence of Gód,
in the líght of the líving.

Psalm 57 (56)

[1] *For the Choirmaster. Intoned like "Do not destroy."*
A Miktam *of David when he fled from Saul into a cave.*

[2] Have mércy on me, Gód, have mércy,
for in yóu my sóul has taken réfuge.
In the shádow of your wíngs I take réfuge,
till the stórms of destrúction pass bý.

[3] I cáll to you, Gód the Most Hígh,
to Gód who provídes for mé.
[4] O sénd from héaven and sáve me,
and pút to shame thóse who assáil me.
O sénd your loving mércy and fáithfulness.

[5] My sóul lies dówn among líons,
who would devóur human préy.
Their téeth are spéars and árrows,
their tóngue a shárpened swórd.
[6] Be exálted, O Gód, above the héavens,
your glóry over áll the éarth!

[7] They láid down a nét for my stéps;
my sóul was bowed dówn.
They dúg a pít in my páth,
but féll in it themsélves.

[8] My héart is réady, O Gód;
my héart is réady.
I will síng, I will síng your práise.
[9] Awáke, my sóul!
Awáke, O lýre and hárp!
I will awáke the dáwn.

[10] I will práise you, Lórd, among the péoples,
among the nátions sing psálms to you,
[11] for your mércy réaches to the héavens,
and your trúth to the skíes.
[12] Be exálted, O Gód, above the héavens;
may your glóry shine on áll the éarth!

Psalm 58 *(57)*

[1] *For the Choirmaster. Intoned like "Do not destroy."*
A Miktam *of David.*

[2] Do you trúly decrée the ríght,
you who hóld divine pówer?
Do you judge ríghtly the húman ráce?
[3] No, in your héarts you devíse iníquities;
your hands déal out víolence to the lánd.

[4] The wícked go astráy from the wómb;
déviant from bírth, they speak líes.
[5] Their vénom is líke the vénom of the snáke;
they are líke a deaf víper stópping its éars,
[6] lést it should héar the snáke-charmer's vóice,
the vóice of the skíllful déaler in spélls.

[7] O Gód, break the téeth in their móuths;
tear out the fángs of these líons, O Lórd!
[8] Let them vánish like wáter that rúns awáy;
let them wíther like gráss that is tródden
underfóot.
[9] Let them bé like the snáil that dissólves into slíme,
like a wóman's míscarriage that néver sees the sún.

[10] Before they pút forth thórns, like a brámble,
let them be swépt away, gréen wood or drý!
[11] The ríghteous shall rejóice at the síght of véngeance;
they shall báthe their féet in the blóod of the wícked.
[12] Péople shall say: "Trúly, the ríghteous are rewárded.
Trúly there ís a God who júdges on éarth."

Psalm 59 *(58)*

[1] *For the Choirmaster. Intoned like "Do not destroy."*
A Miktam *of David when Saul sent men to keep watch on his house and kill him.*

[2] Réscue me, Gód, from my fóes;
protéct me from thóse who attáck me.
[3] O réscue me from thóse who do évil,
and sáve me from thóse who are blóodthirsty.

[4] See, they líe in wáit for my lífe;
the stróng band togéther agáinst me.
For no offénse, no sín of mine, O Lórd,
[5] for no guílt of mine they rúsh to take their stánd.

Awáke! Come to méet me, and sée!
[6] Lord God of hósts, you are Ísrael's Gód.
Róuse yourself and púnish the nátions;
show no mércy to évil tráitors.
[7] Each évening théy come báck;
howling like dógs, they róam about the cíty.

[8] Sée how their móuths utter ínsults;
their líps are like shárpened swórds.
"For whó," they sáy, "will héar us?"
[9] But yóu, Lord, will láugh them to scórn.
You make a móckery of áll the nátions.

[10] O my Stréngth, for yóu will I wátch,
for yóu, O Gód, are my strónghold,
[11] the God who shóws me fáithful lóve.

Now Gód will procéed befóre me,
Gód will let me lóok upon my fóes.
[12] Do not kíll them lest my péople forgét;
róut them by your pówer, lay them lów.

It is yóu, O Lórd, who are our shíeld.
[13] For the síns of their móuths and the wórds of
their líps,
lét them be cáught in their príde;
for the cúrses and líes that they spéak.

[14] Consúme them, consúme them in ánger
till they áre no móre.
Then they will knów that Gód is the rúler
over Jácob and the énds of the éarth.

[15] Each évening théy come báck;
they howl like dógs and róam about the cíty.
[16] They prówl in séarch of fóod;
they grówl till they háve their fíll.

[17] As for mé, I will síng of your stréngth,
and accláim your faithful lóve in the mórning,
for yóu have béen my strónghold,
a réfuge in the dáy of my distréss.

[18] O my Stréngth, to yóu I will sing práise,
for yóu, O Gód, are my strónghold,
the God who shóws me fáithful lóve.

Psalm 60 *(59)*

[1] *For the Choirmaster. Intoned like "The Lily of Testimony." A* Miktam *of David for instruction when he went out against the Aram-Haharaim and Aram-Sobah, and when Joab returned to Edom and defeated twelve thousand in the Valley of Salt.*

[3] O Gód, you have rejécted us, and bróken us.
You have been ángry; come báck to ús.

[4] You have máde the earth quáke, torn it ópen.
Repáir what is sháttered, for it swáys.
[5] You have inflícted hárdships on your péople,
made us drínk a wíne that dázed us.

[6] For those who féar you, you gáve the sígnal
to flée from the fáce of the bów.
[7] With your right hánd, grant salvátion, and give ánswer,
that thóse whom you lóve may be frée.

[8] From the sánctuary Gód has spóken:
"I will exúlt, and divíde the land of Shéchem;
I will méasure out the válley of Súccoth.

[9] "Mine is Gílead, míne is Manásseh;
Éphraim I táke for my hélmet,
Júdah ís my scépter.

[10] "Móab ís my wáshbowl;
on Édom I will cást my shóe.
Over Philístia I will shóut in tríumph."

[11] But who will léad me to the fórtified cíty?
Whó will bríng me to Édom?
[12] Have yóu, O Gód, rejécted us?
Will you márch with our ármies no lónger?

[13] Gíve us áid against the fóe,
for húman hélp is váin.
[14] With Gód wé shall do brávely,
and Gód will trámple down our fóes.

Psalm 61 (60)

[1] *For the Choirmaster. With stringed instruments.*
Of David.

[2] Lísten, O Gód, to my crý!
Atténd to my práyer!
[3] From the énd of the éarth I cáll you;
my héart is fáint.

Sét me hígh upon the róck
too hígh for me to réach,
[4] you, my réfuge and míghty tówer
agáinst the fóe.

[5] Then will I dwéll in your ténf forév er,
and híde in the shélter of your wíngs.
[6] For yóu, O God, have héard my vóws;
yóu have gíven me the héritage
of thóse who féar your náme.

[7] Day upon dáy you will ádd to the kíng;
his yéars as áge upon áge.
[8] May he éver sit enthróned before Gód:
bid mércy and trúth be his protéction.
[9] So I will síng to your náme forév er,
and dáy after dáy fulfill my vóws.

Psalm 62 *(61)*

[1] *For the Choirmaster. Intoned like Jeduthun. A Psalm of David.*

[2] In God alóne is my sóul at rést,
my salvátion cómes from the Lórd.
[3] God alóne is my róck, my salvátion,
my fórtress; I shall nót greatly fálter.

[4] How lóng will you attáck one alóne,
break dówn your víctim,
as you wóuld a tóttering wáll,
or a túmbling fénce?

[5] Their plan is ónly to bring dówn someone of próminence;
they take pléasure in líes.
With their móuth they útter bléssing,
but in their héart they cúrse.

[6] Be at rést, my sóul, in God alóne,
from whóm comes my hópe.
[7] God alóne is my róck, my salvátion,
my fórtress; Í shall not fálter.

[8] In Gód is my salvátion and my glóry,
my róck of stréngth;
in Gód is my réfuge.
[9] Trúst at all tímes, O péople;
pour out your héarts to Gód, our réfuge.

[10] The chíldren of Ádam are a bréath,
an illúsion, péople of ránk.
Pláced on the scáles, they ríse;
they áll weigh léss than a bréath.

[11] Do not pút your trúst in oppréssion,
nor vain hópes on plúnder.
Éven if ríches incréase,
set not your héart on thém.

[12] For Gód has said ónly one thíng;
only twó have I héard:
that to Gód alóne belongs pówer,
[13] and to yóu, Lord, fáithful lóve;
and thát you repáy each of ús
accórding to our déeds.

Psalm 63 *(62)*

[1] *A Psalm of David when he was in the desert of Judah.*

[2] O Gód, you are my Gód; at dawn I séek you;
for yóu my sóul is thírsting.
For yóu my flésh is píning,
like a drý, weary lánd without wáter.
[3] I have cóme before yóu in the hóly place,
to behóld your stréngth and your glóry.

[4] Your faithful lóve is bétter than lífe;
my líps will spéak your práise.
[5] I will bléss you áll my lífe;
in your náme I will líft up my hánds.
[6] My sóul shall be fílled as with a bánquet;
with joyful líps, my móuth shall práise you.

[7] When I remémber you upón my béd,
I muse on yóu through the wátches of the níght.
[8] For yóu have béen my stréngth;
in the shádow of your wíngs I rejóice.
[9] My sóul clings fást to yóu;
yóur right hánd uphólds me.

[10] Those who séek to destróy my lífe
shall go dówn to the dépths of the éarth.
[11] Pút to the pówer of the swórd,
they shall be léft as préy for the jáckals.

[12] But the kíng shall rejóice in Gód;
all that swéar by the Lórd shall exúlt,
for the móuth of líars shall be sílenced.

Psalm 64 *(63)*

[1] *For the Choirmaster. A Psalm of David.*

[2] Hear, O Gód, the vóice of my compláint;
guard my lífe from dréad of the fóe.
[3] From the assémbly of the wícked, híde me,
from the thróng of thóse who do évil.

[4] They shárpen their tóngues like swórds.
They áim bitter wórds like árrows,
[5] to shóot at the ínnocent from ámbush,
shóoting súddenly and féarlessly.

[6] Holding fírm in their évil cóurse,
they conspíre to lay sécret snáres.
They are sáying, "Whó will sée us?
[7] Whó can séarch out our crímes?"

They have hátched their wícked plóts,
and bróught their plóts to perféction.
How profóund the dépths of the héart!

[8] Gód will shóot them with árrows,
and déal them súdden wóunds.
[9] Their own tóngue will bríng them to rúin;
all who sée them will sháke their héads.

[10] Thén will áll be afráid;
they will téll what Gód has dóne.
Théy will pónder God's déeds.
[11] The ríghteous will rejóice in the Lórd,
in whóm they shall take réfuge.
All úpright héarts will glóry.

Psalm 65 (64)

[1] *For the Choirmaster. A Psalm of David. A Song.*

[2] Praise is dúe to you in Zíon, O Gód.
To you we páy our vóws in Jerúsalem,
[3] yóu who héar our práyer.
To yóu all flésh will cóme.
[4] Our evil déeds are too héavy for ús,
but only yóu can párdon our transgréssions.

[5] Blessed the óne whom you chóose and cáll
to dwéll in your cóurts.
We are fílled with the góod things of your hóuse,
of your hóly témple.

[6] With wóndrous delíverance you ánswer us,
O Gód our sávior.
You are the hópe of áll the éarth,
and of fár distant séas.

[7] You estáblish the móuntains with your stréngth;
you are gírded with pówer.
[8] You stíll the róaring of the séas,
the róaring of their wáves,
and the túmult of the péoples.

[9] Distant péoples stánd in áwe
at your wóndrous déeds.
The lánds of súnrise and súnset
you fíll with your jóy.

[10] You vísit the éarth, give it wáter;
you fíll it with ríches.
God's éver-flowing ríver brims óver
to prepáre the gráin.

And thús it is yóu who prepáre it:
[11] you drénch its fúrrows;
you lével it, sóften it with shówers;
you bléss its grówth.

[12] You crówn the yéar with your bóunty,
and abúndance flóws in your páthways.
[13] The pástures of the désert overflów,
and the hílls are gírded with jóy,

[14] The méadows are clóthed with flócks,
and the válleys are décked with whéat.
They shóut for jóy, and even síng!

Psalm 66 *(65)*

[1] *For the Choirmaster. A Song. A Psalm.*

Cry out with jóy to Gód, all the éarth;
[2] O síng to the glóry of God's náme.
O rénder glórious práise.
[3] Say to Gód, "How áwesome your déeds!

Becáuse of the gréatness of your stréngth,
your énemies cówer befóre you.
[4] Before yóu all the éarth shall bow dówn,
shall síng to you, síng to your náme!"

[5] Come and sée the wórks of Gód:
awesome déeds among the chíldren of Ádam.
[6] God túrned the séa into dry lánd;
they pássed through the ríver on fóot.

Thére did we rejóice in the Lórd,
[7] who rúles forév er with míght,
whose éyes keep wátch on the nátions:
let rébels not exált themsélves.

[8] O péoples, bléss our Gód;
let our vóice of práise resóund,
[9] to the Gód who gave lífe to our sóuls
and képt our féet from stúmbling.

[10] For yóu, O Gód, have tésted us,
you have tríed us as sílver is tríed;
[11] you léd us, Gód, into the snáre;
you láid a heavy búrden on our bácks.

[12] You let péople ride óver our héads;
we wént through fíre and through wáter,
but then you bróught us to a pláce of plénty.

[13] Burnt óffering I bríng to your hóuse;
to yóu I will páy my vóws,
[14] the vóws which my líps have úttered,
which my móuth decláred in my distréss.

[15] I will óffer you burnt ófferings of fátlings
with the smóke of sácrificial ráms.
I will óffer búllocks and góats.

[16] Come and héar, áll who fear Gód;
I will téll what God has dóne for my sóul.
[17] To the Lórd I críed alóud,
with exaltátion réady on my tóngue.

[18] Had I chérished évil in my héart,
the Lórd would nót have lístened.
[19] But trúly Gód has lístened,
and has héeded the vóice of my práyer.
[20] Blest be Gód, who did nót reject my práyer,
nor withhóld from me fáithful lóve.

Psalm 67 (66)

[1] *For the Choirmaster. With string instruments.*
A Psalm. A Song.

[2] May Gód be grácious and bléss us.
Let your fáce shed its líght upón us.
[3] So will your wáys be knówn upon éarth
and all nátions léarn your salvátion.

[4] Let the péoples práise you, O Gód;
let áll the péoples práise you.

[5] Let the nátions be glád and shout for jóy,
with úprightness you rúle the péoples;
you guíde the nátions on éarth.

[6] Let the péoples práise you, O Gód;
let áll the péoples práise you.

[7] The éarth has yíelded its frúit
for Gód, our Gód, has bléssed us.
[8] May Gód still gíve us his bléssing,
and be revéred to all the énds of the éarth.

Psalm 68 *(67)*

[1] *For the Choirmaster. Of David. A Psalm. A Song.*

[2] Let Gód aríse; let all fóes be scáttered.
Let thóse who háte the Lord flée from the présence.
[3] As smoke is dríven awáy, so dríve them awáy;
like wáx that mélts befóre the fíre,
so the wícked shall pérish at the présence of Gód.

[4] But the ríghteous shall rejóice at the présence of Gód;
théy shall exúlt with glád rejóicing.
[5] O síng to Gód; make músic to God's náme.
Extól the Óne who rídes on the clóuds,
whose náme is the Lórd, in whose présence we exúlt.

[6] Father of órphans, defénder of wídows:
such is Gód in the hóly pláce.
[7] God gives the désolate a hóme to dwéll in,
and leads the prísoners fórth into prospérity,
while rébels must dwéll in a parched lánd.

[8] O Gód, when you went fórth before your péople,
when you márched acróss the désert,
[9] the earth trémbled, heavens póured down ráin
at the présence of Gód, the God of Sínai,
at the présence of Gód, the God of Ísrael.

[10] You póured down, O Gód, a génerous ráin;
when your héritage lánguished, yóu restóred it.
[11] It was thére that your flóck begán to dwéll.
In your góodness, O Gód, you províded for the
póor.

[12] The Lórd annóunces the commánd;
a mighty thróng of máidens bears good tídings:
[13] "Kíngs with their ármies will flée, will flée,
and at hóme the wómen alréady share the spóil,
[14] though théy are at rést among the shéepfolds:

They are cóvered with sílver as the wíngs of a
dóve,
its féathers brílliant with shíning góld.
[15] When the Almíghty scatters kíngs on the
móuntain,
it is like snów that whítens Mount Zálmon."

[16] O gódly móuntain, móuntain of Báshan;
O mány-peaked móuntain, móuntain of Báshan!
[17] Why lóok with énvy, you mány-peaked
móuntain,
at the móuntain where Gód has desíred to dwéll?
It is thére that the Lórd shall dwéll forévér.

[18] The cháriots of Gód are thóusands upon thóusands.
The Lórd has cóme from Sínai to the hóly place.
[19] You have ascénded on hígh, leading captívity
cáptive;
recéiving péople as tríbute,
so that éven the rebéllious may dwéll near the
LORD Gód.

[20] Dáy after dáy, may the Lórd be blést
who béars our búrdens; Gód is our sávior.
[21] This Gód of óurs is a Gód who sáves.
The LORD our Lórd provídes an escápe from déath.
[22] And Gód will smíte the héads of fóes,
the hairy crówn of thóse who wálk about in guílt.

[23] The Lord sáid, "I will bríng them báck from
Báshan;
I will bríng them báck from the dépth of the séa.
[24] Thén you will báthe your féet in their blóod,
and the tóngues of your dógs take their sháre of
the fóe."

[25] They sée your sólemn procéssion, O Gód,
the procéssion of my Gód, of my kíng, to the hóly
place:
[26] the síngers in the fórefront, the musícians coming
lást;
betwéen them, máidens sóunding their tímbrels.

[27] "In the sácred assémbly, bléss God, the LÓRD,
O yóu, from the fóuntain of Ísrael."
[28] There is Bénjamin, léast of the tríbes, at the héad;
Júdah's prínces, a míghty thróng;
Zébulun's prínces, Náphtali's prínces.

[29] Súmmon fórth your míght, O Gód;
your míght, O Gód, which you have shówn for ús.
[30] From your témple hígh in Jerúsalem,
kings will cóme to you brínging their tríbute.

[31] Rebúke the wild béast that dwélls in the réeds,
the hérd of búlls among the cálves of the peoples:
They próstrate themsélves with plátes of sílver.
Scátter the nátions who delíght in wárs.
[32] Rich mérchants will máke their wáy from Égypt;
Ethiópia will strétch out her hánds to Gód.

[33] You kíngdoms of the éarth, sing to Gód, praise
the Lórd
[34] who rídes on the héavens, the áncient héavens.
Behóld, the Lord thúnders with a míghty vóice.

[35] Cóme, let us acknówledge the pówer of Gód,
whose glóry is on Ísrael; whose míght is in the
skíes.
[36] Áwesome are yóu, O Gód, in your hóly place,
Yoú who are the Gód of Ísrael.
You give stréngth and pówer to your péople.
Blést bé Gód!

Psalm 69 *(68)*

[1] *For the Choirmaster. Intoned like "Lilies."*
Of David.

[2] Sáve me, O Gód, for the wáters
have rísen to my néck.
[3] I have súnk into the múd of the déep,
where there ís no fóothold.
I have éntered the wáters of the déep,
where the flóod overwhélms me.

[4] I am wéaried with crýing alóud;
my thróat is párched.
My éyes are wásted awáy
with wáiting for my Gód.

[5] More númerous than the háirs on my héad
are those who háte me without cáuse.
Míghty are thóse who attáck me,
énemies with líes.
Whát I have néver stólen,
hów can I restóre?

[6] O Gód, you knów my fólly;
from you my síns are not hídden.
[7] May those who hópe in you nót be shámed
because of mé, O Lord of hósts;
may those who séek you nót be disgráced
because of mé, O God of Ísrael.

[8] It is for yóu that I súffer táunts,
that sháme has cóvered my fáce.
[9] To my own kín I have becóme an óutcast,
a stránger to the chíldren of my móther.
[10] Zéal for your hóuse consúmes me,
and táunts against yóu fall on mé.

[11] When my sóul wept bítterly in fásting,
they máde it a táunt agáinst me.
[12] When I máde my clóthing sáckcloth,
I becáme a repróach to thém,
[13] the góssip of thóse at the gátes,
the théme of drúnkards' sóngs.

[14] But I práy to yóu, O Lórd,
at an accéptable tíme.
In your great mércy, ánswer me, O Gód,
with your fáithful salvátion.

[15] Rescue mé from the míre, lest I sínk.
From thóse who háte me, delíver me,
and from the wáters of the déep,
[16] lest the wáves overwhélm me.
Let nót the déep engúlf me,
nor the pít close its móuth on mé.

[17] Lord, ánswer, for your lóve is kínd;
in your abúndant compássion, turn towards mé.
[18] Do not híde your fáce from your sérvant;
answer me quíckly, for Í am in distréss.
[19] Come clóse to my sóul and redéem me;
ránsom me becáuse of my fóes.

[20] You know my táunts, my sháme, my dishónor;
my oppréssors are áll befóre you.
[21] Táunts have bróken my héart;
hére I ám in ánguish.
I looked for sólace, but thére was nóne;
for consólers—not óne could I fínd.

[22] For fóod they gáve me gáll;
in my thírst they gave me vínegar to drínk.
[23] Let their táble be a snáre to thém,
and for their fríends, a tráp.
[24] Let their éyes grow dím and blínd;
let their límbs contínually trémble.

[25] Pour óut your ánger upón them;
let your búrning fúry overtáke them.
[26] Lét their cámp be left désolate;
let nó one dwéll in their ténts:
[27] for they pérsecute óne whom you strúck;
they incréase the pain of óne whom you
wóunded.

[28] Chárge them with guílt upon guílt;
let them háve no sháre in your jústice.
[29] Blot them óut from the bóok of the líving;
do not enróll them amóng the ríghteous.

[30] As for mé in my póverty and páin,
let your salvátion, O Gód, raise me úp.
[31] Then I will práise God's náme with a sóng;
I will glórify the Lórd with thanksgíving:
[32] a gift pléasing the LÓRD more than óxen,
more than a búll with hórns and hóoves.

[33] The póor when they sée it will be glád,
and Gód-seeking héarts will revíve;
[34] for the LÓRD atténds the néedy,
and dóes not spurn thóse in their cháins.
[35] Let the héavens and the éarth give práise to Gód,
the seas and éverything that móves in thém.

[36] For Gód will bring salvátion to Zíon,
and rebuíld the cíties of Júdah,
and théy shall dwéll there in posséssion.
[37] The chíldren of God's sérvants shall inhérit it;
those who lóve the Lord's náme shall dwéll there.

Psalm 70 (69)

[1] *For the Choirmaster. Of David. A Memorial.*

[2] O Gód, cóme to my assístance;
O Lórd, make háste to hélp me!
[3] Lét there be sháme and confúsion
on thóse who séek my lífe.

O lét them turn báck in confúsion,
who delíght in my hárm;
[4] let them túrn becáuse of their sháme,
who jéer at me and móck.

[5] O lét there be rejóicing and gládness
for áll who séek you.
Let them sáy forever, "Gód is gréat,"
who lóve your saving hélp.

[6] As for mé, who am wrétched and póor,
hasten to mé, O Gód.
Yóu are my réscuer, my hélp;
O Lórd, do not deláy.

Psalm 71 (70)

[1] In yóu, O Lórd, I take réfuge;
let me néver be pút to sháme.
[2] In your ríghteousness, réscue me, frée me;
inclíne your éar to me and sáve me.

[3] Be my róck, my cónstant réfuge,
a míghty strónghold to sáve me,
for yóu are my róck, my strónghold.
[4] My God, frée me from the hánd of the wícked,
from the gríp of the unjúst, of the oppréssor.

[5] It is yóu, O Lórd, who are my hópe,
my trúst, O Lórd, from my yóuth.
[6] On yóu I have léaned from my bírth;
it was yóu who tóok me from my móther's wómb.
At all tímes I gíve you práise.

[7] My fáte has filled mány with áwe,
but yóu are my míghty réfuge.
[8] My móuth is fílled with your práise,
with your glóry, áll the day lóng.
[9] Do not rejéct me nów that I am óld;
when my stréngth fails dó not forsáke me.

[10] For my énemies are spéaking abóut me;
those who wátch me take cóunsel togéther.
[11] They say Gód has forsáken mé;
they can séize me, for nó one will sáve me.
[12] O Gód, do not stáy far óff;
O my Gód, make háste to hélp me!

[13] Let them be pút to sháme and consúmed,
thóse who séek my lífe.
Let them be cóvered with sháme and confúsion,
thóse who séek to hárm me.

[14] But as for mé, I will álways hópe,
and práise you móre and móre.
[15] My móuth will téll of your ríghteousness,
and áll the day lóng of your salvátion,
though I can néver téll it áll.

[16] I will cóme with práise of your míght, O Lórd;
I will cáll to mínd your ríghteousness,
yóurs, O Lórd, alóne.

[17] O Gód, you have táught me from my yóuth,
and I procláim your wónders stíll.
[18] Even tíll I am óld and gray-héaded,
dó not forsáke me, O Gód.

Let me téll of your míghty árm
to évery cóming generátion;
[19] your stréngth and your jústice, O Gód,
réach to the híghest héavens.
It is yóu who have wórked such wónders.
O Gód, whó is like yóu?

[20] You have máde me wítness many tróubles and
évils,
but you will gíve me báck my lífe.
You will ráise me from the dépths of the éarth;
[21] you will exált me and consóle me agáin.

[22] So I will gíve you thánks on the lýre
for your fáithfulness, Ó my Gód.
To yóu will I síng with the hárp,
to yóu, the Hóly One of Ísrael.
[23] When I síng to you, my líps shall shout for jóy,
and my sóul, which yóu have redéemed.

[24] And áll the day lóng my tóngue
shall téll the tále of your ríghteousness,
for they are pút to sháme and disgráced,
thóse who sóught to hárm me.

Psalm 72 (71)

[1] *Of Solomon.*

O Gód, give your júdgment to the kíng,
to a king's són your ríghteousness,
[2] that he may júdge your péople in ríghteousness,
and your póor in right júdgment.

[3] May the móuntains bring forth péace for the
péople,
and the hílls bear péace in ríghteousness.
[4] May he defénd the póor of the péople,
and sáve the chíldren of the néedy,
and crúsh the oppréssor.

[5] He shall endúre like the sún and the móon
through áll generátions.
[6] He shall descénd like ráin on the méadow,
like shówers that wáter the éarth.
[7] In his dáys shall ríghteousness flóurish,
and great péace till the móon is no móre.

[8] He shall rúle from séa to séa,
from the Ríver to the bóunds of the éarth.
[9] Let the désert dwellers fáll befóre him,
and his énemies líck the dúst.

[10] The kíngs of Társhish and the íslands
shall páy him tríbute.
The kíngs of Shéba and Séba
shall bríng him gífts.
[11] Before hím all kíngs shall fall próstrate,
all nátions shall sérve him.

[12] For he shall réscue the néedy when they crý,
the póor who have nó one to hélp.
[13] He will have píty on the wéak and the néedy,
and save the líves of the néedy.
[14] From oppréssion and víolence he redéems their
lífe;
to him their blóod is déar.

[15] Long may he líve, and the góld of Shéba be gíven
him.
They shall práy for hím without céasing,
and bléss him áll the dáy.

[16] May gráin be abúndant in the lánd,
wáving to the péaks of the móuntains.
May its frúit rústle like Lébanon;
may the péople flóurish in the cíties
like gráss on the éarth.

[17] May his náme endúre forever,
his náme contínue like the sún.
Every tríbe shall be blést in hím,
all nátions shall cáll him bléssed.

* * *

[18] Blést be the LÓRD, God of Ísrael,
who alóne works wónders,
[19] Ever blést the glorious náme of the Lórd.
Let the glóry of Gód fill the éarth.
Amén! Amén!

[20] Here end the Psalms of David, son of Jesse.

BOOK THREE OF THE PSALTER

Psalm 73 (72)

[1] *A Psalm of Asaph.*

How góod is Gód to Ísrael,
to thóse who are púre of héart!
[2] As for mé, my féet came clóse to stúmbling;
my stéps had álmost slípped,
[3] for I was fílled with énvy of the próud,
when I sáw how the wícked prósper.

[4] For thém there áre no páins;
their bódies are sóund and sléek.
[5] They do not sháre in péople's búrdens;
théy are not strícken like óthers.

[6] So they wéar their príde like a nécklace;
they clóthe themsélves with víolence.
[7] With folds of fát, their éyes protrúde.
With imaginátion their héarts overflów.

[8] They scóff; they spéak with málice.
From on hígh they thréaten oppréssion.
[9] They have sét their móuths in the héavens,
and their tóngues are róaming the éarth.

[10] So the péople túrn to thém
and drínk in áll their wórds.
[11] Thús they say, "Hów can God knów?
Dóes the Most Hígh have any knówledge?"
[12] Lóok at them, súch are the wícked;
ever prósperous, they grów in wéalth.

[13] How úseless to kéep my heart púre,
and wásh my hánds in ínnocence,
[14] when I was strícken áll day lóng,
suffered púnishment with éach new mórning.
[15] Then I sáid, "If I should spéak like thát,
I should betráy the ráce of your chíldren."

[16] I stróve to fáthom this próblem,
too hárd for my mínd to understánd,
[17] until I éntered the hóly place of Gód,
and cáme to discérn their énd.

[18] How slíppery the páths on which you sét them;
you máke them fáll to destrúction.
[19] How súddenly they cóme to their rúin,
swept awáy, destróyed by térrors.
[20] Like a dréam one wákes from, O Lórd,
when you wáke you dismíss them as phántoms.

[21] And só when my héart grew embíttered,
and I was píerced to the dépths of my béing,
[22] I was stúpid and did nót understánd;
I was líke a béast in your síght.

[23] As for mé, I was álways in your présence;
you were hólding mé by my right hánd.
[24] By your cóunsel yóu will guíde me,
and thén you will léad me to glóry.

[25] What élse have I in héaven but yóu?
Apart from yóu, I want nóthing on éarth.
[26] My flésh and my héart waste awáy;
Gód is the stréngth of my héart,
my pórtion foréver.

[27] Surely, thóse who are fár from you pérish;
you put an énd to all thóse who are unfáithful.
[28] For mé to be near Gód is góod;
I have máde the Lord Góᴅ my réfuge.
Í will procláim your wórks
at the gátes of dáughter Zíon.

Psalm 74 (73)

[1] *A* Maskil *of Asaph.*

Whý, O Gód, have you cást us off forévér?
Why does your ánger bláze at the shéep of your pásture?
[2] Remémber your flóck which you cláimed long agó,
the tríbe you redéemed to be your ówn possession,
this móuntain of Zíon where you máde your dwélling.

[3] Turn your stéps to these pláces that are útterly rúined!
The énemy has laid wáste the whóle of the hóly place.
[4] Your fóes have made úproar in the mídst of your assémbly;
they have sét up their émblems as tókens thére.
[5] They have wíelded their áxes on hígh,
as at the éntrance to a gróve of trées.

[6] Théy have bróken down áll the cárvings;
they have strúck togéther with hátchet and píckaxe.
[7] They have sét your hóly place on fíre;
they have rázed and profáned the abóde of your náme.

[8] They sáid in their héarts, "We will útterly crúsh
them;
we will búrn every shríne of Gód in the lánd."
[9] We do not sée our émblems, nór is there a
próphet;
we have nó one to téll us how lóng it will lást.

[10] How lóng, O Gód, is the énemy to scóff?
Is the fóe to insúlt your náme foréver?
[11] Whý do you hóld back your hánd?
Why do you kéep your ríght hand hídden in
your clóak?

[12] Yet it is Gód who réigns from of óld,
who bestóws salvátion through áll the lánd.
[13] It was yóu who divíded the séa by your míght,
who sháttered the héads of the mónsters in the
séa.

[14] It was yóu who crúshed Levíathan's héads,
and gáve it as fóod to the béasts of the désert.
[15] It was yóu who ópened up spríngs and tórrents;
it was yóu who dríed up éver-flowing rívers.

[16] Yóurs is the dáy and yóurs is the níght;
it was yóu who estáblished the líght and the sún.
[17] It was yóu who fíxed the bóunds of the éarth,
yóu who máde both súmmer and wínter.

[18] Remémber this, O Lórd: the énemy scóffed!
A sénseless péople insúlted your náme!
[19] Do not gíve the sóul of your dóve to the béasts,
nor forgét the lífe of your póor ones forév er.

[20] Lóok to the cóvenant; for cáves in the lánd
are pláces where víolence mákes its hóme.
[21] Do not lét the oppréssed be pút to sháme;
let the póor and the néedy bléss your náme.

[22] Aríse, O Gód, and defénd your cáuse!
Remémber how the sénseless revíle you all the
dáy.
[23] Dó not forgét the clámor of your fóes,
the uncéasing úproar of thóse who defý you.

Psalm 75 (74)

[1] *For the Choirmaster. Intoned like "Do not destroy." A Psalm of Asaph. A Song.*

[2] We give práise to yóu, O Gód;
we give práise, for your náme is néar.
We recóunt your wónderful déeds.

[3] "When I estáblish the appóinted tíme,
then I mysélf will júdge with fáirness.
[4] Though the éarth and all who dwéll in it may róck,
it is Í who set fírm its píllars.

[5] To the bóastful I sáy, 'Do not bóast';
to the wícked, 'Do not fláunt your stréngth,
[6] do not exált your stréngth on hígh.
Do not spéak with ínsolent príde.'"

[7] For néither from the éast nor from the wést,
nor from the désert cómes exaltátion.
[8] For Gód alóne is the júdge,
who humbles óne and exálts anóther.

[9] For in the hánd of the Lórd is a cúp,
full of wíne, both fóaming and spíced.
God póurs it; they dráin it to the drégs;
all the wícked on the éarth must dráin it.
[10] As for mé, I will rejóice foréver,
and sing psálms to the Gód of Jácob.

[11] I shall bréak the stréngth of the wícked,
while the stréngth of the júst will be exálted.

Psalm 76 (75)

[1] *For the Choirmaster. With String Instruments.*
A Psalm of Asaph. A Song.

[2] O Gód, you are renówned in Júdah;
in Ísrael your náme is gréat.
[3] You sét up your tént in Sálem,
and your dwélling pláce in Zíon.
[4] It was thére you bróke the flaming árrows,
the shíeld, the swórd, the ármor.

[5] Resplendent are yóu, more majéstic
than the éverlásting móuntains.
[6] The stouthéarted, despóiled, sank into slúmber;
none of the sóldiers could líft a hánd.
[7] At your thréat, O Gód of Jácob,
hórse and ríder lay stúnned.

[8] Yóu, you alóne, strike térror.
Who can stánd in your présence,
against the míght of your wráth?

[9] You úttered your séntence from the héavens;
the éarth in térror was stíll
[10] when you aróse, O Gód, to júdge,
to sáve all the húmble of the éarth.

[11] For human ráge only sérves to práise you;
you surróund yoursélf with the survívors of
wráth.
[12] Make vóws to the Lórd your Gód and fulfíll
them.
Let all aróund pay tríbute to the Óne who strikes
térror,
[13] who cuts shórt the bréath of léaders,
who strikes térror in the rúlers of the éarth.

***Psalm** 77 (76)*

[1] *For the Choirmaster. Intoned like "Jeduthun."*
Of Asaph. A Psalm.

[2] I crý alóud to Gód,
cry alóud to Gód that I be héard.

[3] In the dáy of my distréss I seek the Lórd.
In the níght my hands are ráised unwéaried;
my sóul refúses cómfort.
[4] As I remémber my Gód, I gróan.
I pónder, and my spírit fáints.

[5] You kéep my éyes from clósing.
I am tróubled, unáble to spéak.
[6] I thínk of the dáys of long agó,
and remémber the yéars long pást.
[7] At níght I múse within my héart.
I pónder, and my spírit quéstions.

[8] "Will the Lórd rejéct us foréver,
and shów divine fávor no móre?
[9] Has God's fáithful kíndness vánished foréver?
Has the prómise cóme to an énd,
[10] or God's mércy béen forgótten,
or compássion withdráwn in ánger?"

[11] I said, "Thís is what cáuses my gríef:
that the right hánd of the Most Hígh has chánged."
[12] I remémber the déeds of the Lórd,
I remémber your wónders of óld;
[13] I múse on áll your wórks,
and pónder your míghty déeds.

[14] Your wáy, O Gód, is hóly.
What gód is as gréat as our Gód?
[15] Yóu are the Gód who works wónders.
Among the péoples you shówed your pówer.
[16] Your strong árm redéemed your péople,
the descéndants of Jácob and Jóseph.

[17] The wáters sáw you, O Gód;
the wáters sáw you and ánguished.
Yes, the dépths were móved to trémble.
[18] The clóuds poured dówn with ráin.
The skíes sent fórth their vóice;
your árrows fláshed to and fró.

[19] Your thúnderous vóice was in the whírlwind;
your fláshes líghted up the wórld.
The éarth was móved and trémbled.
[20] Your wáy was thróugh the séa,
your páth through the míghty wáters,
but the tráce of your stéps was not séen.

[21] You guíded your péople like a flóck
by the hánd of Móses and Áaron.

Psalm 78 *(77)*

[1] *A* Maskil *of Asaph.*

Give éar, my péople, to my téaching;
incline your éar to the wórds of my móuth.
[2] I will ópen my móuth in a párable
and útter hidden léssons of the pást.

[3] The thíngs we have héard and understóod,
the thíngs our párents have tóld us,
[4] thése we will not híde from our children
but will téll them to the néxt generátion:
the glóries and the míght of the Lórd,
and the márvelous déeds that have been dóne.

[5] God estáblished a decrée in Jácob,
and sét up a láw in Ísrael.
Our fórebears were gíven a commánd
to máke it knówn to their chíldren,
[6] that the néxt generátion might knów it,
the chíldren yét to be bórn.

They should aríse and decláre it to their chíldren,
[7] that they should sét their hópe in Gód,
and néver forgét God's déeds,
but kéep every óne of the commándments,

[8] So that théy might not bé like their fórebears,
a defíant and rebéllious generátion,
a generátion whose héart was fíckle,
whose spírit was not fáithful to Gód.

[9] The Éphraimites, ármed with the bów,
turned báck on the dáy of báttle.
[10] They fáiled to kéep God's cóvenant,
refused to wálk accórding to the láw.

[11] They forgót the things Gód had dóne,
the wóndrous wórks that had been shówn them,
[12] wonders wórked in the síght of their fórebears,
in Égypt, in the pláins of Zóan.

[13] God divíded the séa and led them thróugh,
and made the wáters stand úp like a wáll.
[14] By dáy the Lord léd them with a clóud;
throughout the níght, with a líght of fíre.

[15] The Lord splít the rócks in the désert,
gave them pléntiful drínk, as from the déep,
[16] making stréams flow óut from the róck,
and wáters flow dówn like rívers.

[17] Yet stíll they sínned against Gód,
rebelled agáinst the Most Hígh in the désert.
[18] In their héart they put Gód to the tést
by demánding the fóod they cráved.

[19] They spóke against Gód and sáid:
"Can Gód spread a táble in the wílderness?
[20] Behóld, it was the Lórd who struck the róck:
water gushed fórth and swept dówn in tórrents.
But cán the Most Hígh give us bréad?
Can Gód provide méat for the péople?"

[21] Upon héaring this, the LÓRD was ángry.
A fíre was kíndled against Jácob;
divine ánger róse against Ísrael.
[22] For they hád no fáith in Gód,
did not trúst the saving pówer of the Lórd.

[23] Yet God commánded the clóuds abóve,
and ópened the gátes of héaven,
[24] rained down mánna for thém to éat,
and gáve them bréad from héaven.

[25] Human béings ate the bréad of ángels;
the Lord sént them an abúndance of fóod,
[26] stirring úp the east wínd in the héavens,
and dirécting the sóuth wind with míght.

[27] The Lord rained flésh upón them like dúst,
winged fówl like the sánds of the séa,
[28] letting it fáll in the mídst of their cámp,
and áll aróund their ténts.

[29] So they áte and hád their fíll,
whát they cráved, God gáve them.

[30] But befóre they had sáted their húnger,
while the fóod was stíll in their móuths,
[31] God róse in ánger agáinst them
and sléw the stróngest amóng them,
struck dówn the flówer of Ísrael.

[32] Despíte all this, they képt on sínning;
they fáiled to belíeve divine wónders.
[33] So God énded their dáys like a bréath,
and their yéars in súdden térror.

[34] When they were sláin, then they sóught the
Lórd;
repénted and éarnestly sought Gód.
[35] They would remémber that Gód was their róck,
Gód the Most Hígh their redéemer.

[36] Yet they decéived the Lórd with their móuths;
they líed with their tóngues.
[37] For their héarts were not stéadfast toward Gód;
théy were not fáithful to the cóvenant.

[38] Yet Gód who is fúll of compássion
forgáve them their sín and spáred them,
so óften héld back divine ánger,
and did nót stir up áll godly ráge.
[39] God remémbered they were ónly flésh,
a breath that pásses, néver to retúrn.

[40] They rebélled against God óften in the désert,
and cáused the Lord páin in the wásteland!
[41] Yet agáin they túrned and tested Gód;
they provóked the Hóly One of Ísrael.

[42] They fáiled to remémber God's déeds
on the dáy they were redéemed from the fóe,
[43] when sígns were perfórmed in Égypt,
and wónders in the pláins of Zóan.

[44] The Lord túrned their rívers into blóod;
they cóuld not drínk from their stréams.
[45] God sent swárms of flíes to devóur them,
and frógs to destróy them;
[46] gáve their cróps to ínsects,
the frúit of their lábor to the lócust.

[47] The Lord destróyed their vínes with háil,
their sýcamore trées with fróst;
[48] gáve up their cáttle to háil,
their hérds to dárts of líghtning.

[49] God unléashed on them the héat of heaven's
ánger,
fúry, ráge and hávoc,
a tróop of destróying ángels.

[50] God léveled a páth for his ánger,
and did not spáre their líves from déath,
but gáve their lívestock to the plágue.
[51] The Lord strúck all the fírstborn in Égypt,
the first vígor of yóuth from the dwéllings of Hám.

[52] Then God bróught forth the péople like shéep,
léd them like a flóck in the désert,
[53] led them sáfely with nóthing to féar,
while the séa engúlfed their fóes.

[54] So the Lord bróught them to the hóly lánd,
to the móuntain wón by God's right hánd,
[55] dríving out the nátions befóre them,
and appórtioning to éach their héritage.
The tribes of Ísrael were séttled in their ténts.

[56] With defíance they tésted God Most Hígh;
they refúsed to obéy divine decrées.
[57] They stráyed as fáithless as their fórebears;
like a tréacherous bów, betrayed the Lórd.
[58] With their high pláces they provóked God to
wráth,
to jéalousy by sérving their ídols.

[59] God héard this and was fílled with fúry;
God útterly rejécted Ísrael,
[60] forsáking the dwélling place at Shíloh,
the tént where God dwélt with human béings.
[61] God gáve the árk into captívity,
divine spléndor to the hánds of the fóe.

[62] God gáve up these péople to the swórd,
showing ánger agáinst these chósen ones.
[63] So fíre devóured their young mén,
their máidens had no wédding sóngs;
[64] their príests were cut dówn by the swórd,
and their wídows máde no lamént.

[65] Then the Lórd awóke as if from sléep,
like a wárrior máddened by wíne,
[66] stríking the fóes from behínd,
and pútting them to sháme foréver.

[67] The Lord rejécted the tént of Jóseph,
and did not chóose the tríbe of Éphraim,
[68] but chóse the tríbe of Júdah,
the belóved móuntain of Zíon,
[69] buílding its shríne like the héavens,
or like the éarth which is fóunded foréver.

[70] And Gód chose Dávid as a sérvant,
and tóok him awáy from the shéepfolds.
[71] From the cáre of the éwes God bróught him
to be shépherd for the péople of Jácob,
over Ísrael, God's ówn posséssion.
[72] He ténded them with blámeless héart;
with his skíllful hánds he léd them.

Psalm 79 (78)

[1] *A Psalm of Asaph.*

O Gód, the nátions have inváded your héritage;
théy have profáned your hóly témple.
They have máde Jerúsalem a héap of rúins.
[2] They have hánded óver the bódies of your
sérvants
as fóod to féed the bírds of héaven,
and the flésh of your fáithful to the béasts of the
éarth.

[3] They have póured out their blóod like wáter
round Jerúsalem;
nó one is léft to búry the déad.
[4] Wé have becóme the táunt of our néighbors,
the móckery and scórn of thóse aróund us.
[5] How lóng, O Lórd? Will you be ángry foréver?
Will your jéalous ánger búrn like fíre?

[6] Póur out your ráge on the nátions,
thóse who dó not knów you,
peoples that dó not cáll upon your náme.
[7] For they devóured the fámily of Jácob
and laid wáste the pláce where they dwéll.

[8] Do nót remémber agáinst us
the guílt of fórmer tímes.
Let your compássion hásten to méet us;
for wé have been bróught very lów.

[9] Hélp us, O Gód our sávior,
for the sáke of the glóry of your náme.
Frée us and forgíve us our síns,
becáuse of your náme.

[10] Whý should the nátions say, "Whére is their Gód?"
Before our éyes make it knówn amóng the nátions
that you avénge the blóod of your sérvants that was shéd.
[11] Let the gróans of the prísoners cóme befóre you,
your strong árm repríeve those condémned to díe.

[12] Pay báck to our néighbors séven times óver
the táunts with whích they táunted you, O Lórd.
[13] Then we, your péople, the flóck of your pásture,
will give you thánks foréver and éver.
From age to áge we will recóunt your práise.

Psalm 80 *(79)*

[1] *For the Choirmaster. Intoned like "Lilies of Testimony." Of Asaph. A Psalm.*

[2] O shépherd of Ísrael, héar us,
yóu who lead Jóseph like a flóck:
enthróned on the chérubim, shine fórth
[3] upon Éphraim, Bénjamin, Manásseh.
Rouse up your míght and cóme to sáve us.

[4] Bríng us báck, O Gód;
let your fáce shine fórth, that wé might be sáved.

[5] How lóng, O Lórd, God of hósts,
will you be ángry at the práyer of your péople?
[6] You have féd them with téars for their bréad,
an abúndance of téars for their drínk.
[7] You have máde us the táunt of our néighbors;
our foes móck us amóng themsélves.

[8] Bríng us báck, O Gód;
let your fáce shine fórth, that wé might be sáved.

[9] You bróught a víne out of Égypt;
you dróve out the nátions and plánted it.
[10] Befóre it you cléared the gróund;
it took róot and filled the lánd.

[11] The móuntains were cóvered with its shádow,
the cédars of Gód with its bóughs.
[12] It strétched out its bránches to the séa;
to the Ríver it strétched out its shóots.

[13] Then whý have you bróken down its wálls?
It is plúcked by all who páss by the wáy.
[14] It is rávaged by the bóar of the fórest,
devóured by the béasts of the fíeld.

[15] God of hósts, turn agáin, we implóre;
look dówn from héaven and sée.

Vísit this víne and protéct it,
[16] the stóck your right hánd has plánted,
the óne you have cláimed for yoursélf.
[17] They have búrnt it with fíre and cut it dówn.
May they pérish at the frówn of your fáce.

[18] May your hánd be on the óne at your right hánd,
the óne you have confírmed as your ówn.
[19] And we shall néver forsáke you agáin;
give us lífe that we may cáll upon your náme.

[20] Bring us báck, O LÓRD God of hósts;
let your fáce shine fórth, that wé might be sáved.

Psalm 81 *(80)*

[1] *For the Choirmaster. Upon* the gittith. *Of Asaph.*

[2] Sing jóyfully to Gód our stréngth,
shout in tríumph to the Gód of Jácob.
[3] Raise a sóng and sóund the tímbrel,
the swéet-sounding lýre with the hárp;
[4] blów the trúmpet at the néw moon,
when the móon is fúll, on our féast.

[5] For thís is a státute in Ísrael,
a commánd of the Gód of Jácob,
[6] who máde it a decrée for Jóseph,
when they went óut from the lánd of Égypt.

A vóice I did not knów said to mé:
[7] "I fréed your shóulder from the búrden;
your hands were fréed from the buílder's básket.
[8] You cálled in distréss and I delívered you.

"I ánswered, concéaled in the thúnder;
at the wáters of Méribah I tésted you.
[9] Lísten, my péople, as I wárn you.
O Ísrael, if ónly you would héed!

[10] "Let there bé no strange gód amóng you,
nor shall you wórship a fóreign gód.
[11] Í am the Lórd your Gód,
who brought you úp from the lánd of Égypt.
Ópen wide your móuth, and I will fíll it.

[12] "But my péople did not héed my vóice,
and Ísrael would nót obéy me.
[13] So I léft them in their stúbbornness of héart,
to fóllow their ówn desígns.

[14] "Ó that my péople would héed me,
that Ísrael would wálk in my wáys!
[15] At ónce I would subdúe their fóes,
turn my hánd agáinst their énemies.

[16] "Those who háte the Lórd would críngе,
and their fáte would lást forévеr.
[17] But Ísrael I would féed with finest whéat,
and sátisfy with hóney from the róck."

Psalm 82 *(81)*

[1] *A Psalm of Asaph.*

God stánds in the divíne assémbly,
in the mídst of the góds gives júdgment.

[2] "How lóng will you júdge unjústly,
and fávor the cáuse of the wícked?
[3] Do jústice for the wéak and the órphan;
give jústice to the póor and afflícted.
[4] Réscue the wéak and the néedy;
set them frée from the hánd of the wícked."

[5] They néither knów nor understánd;
they wálk abóut in dárkness,
and all the éarth's foundátions are sháken.

[6] I have sáid to you, "Yóu are góds,
and áll of you, chíldren of the Móst High.
[7] And yét, like human béings you shall díe;
you shall fáll, like ány earthly rúler."

[8] Aríse, O Gód; judge the éarth!
For áll the nátions are yóurs.

Psalm 83 (82)

[1] *A Song. A Psalm of Asaph.*

[2] O Gód, do nót be sílent;
do not be stíll and unmóved, O Gód.
[3] For your énemies ráise a túmult;
those who háte you líft up their héads.

[4] They plót agáinst your péople,
conspíre against thóse you chérish.
[5] They say, "Cóme, let us destróy them as a nátion;
let not the náme of Ísrael be remémbered."

[6] They conspíre with a síngle mínd;
against yóu they máke a cóvenant:
[7] the cámps of Édom and of Íshmael,
of Móab and Hágar,

[8] Gébal and Ámmon and Ámalek,
Philístia, with the péople of Týre.
[9] Assýria, tóo, is their álly,
and joins hánds with the chíldren of Lót.

[10] Tréat them like Mídian, like Sísera,
like Jábin at the Ríver Kíshon,
[11] thóse who were destróyed at Éndor,
whose bódies rótted on the gróund.

[12] Make their cáptains like Óreb and Zéeb,
all their princes like Zébah and Zalmúnna,
[13] who sáid, "Let us táke the fields of Gód
and máke them our ówn posséssion."

[14] My God, scátter them líke the whírlwind,
dríve them like cháff in the wínd!
[15] As fíre that búrns away the fórest,
as the fláme that sets the móuntains abláze,
[16] dríve them awáy with your témpest,
and fíll them with térror at your stórm.

[17] Cóver their fáces with sháme,
so that they séek your náme, O Lórd.
[18] Shame and térror be théirs foréver.
Lét them be disgráced; let them pérish!

[19] Let them knów that yóu alóne,
yóu whose náme is the Lórd,
are the Most Hígh over áll the éarth.

Psalm 84 *(83)*

[1] *For the Choirmaster. Upon* the gittith. *Of the sons of Korah. A Psalm.*

[2] How lóvely is your dwélling pláce,
O Lórd of hósts.
[3] My sóul is lónging and yéarning
for the cóurts of the Lórd.
My héart and my flésh cry óut
to the líving Gód.

[4] Éven the spárrow finds a hóme,
and the swállow a nést for herself
in which she séts her yóung, at your áltars,
O Lord of hósts, my kíng and my Gód.

[5] Blessed are théy who dwéll in your hóuse,
forévet síngíng your práise.
[6] Blessed the péople whose stréngth is in yóu,
whose héarts are sét on the pílgrimage.

[7] As they gó through the Báca Válley,
they máke it a pláce of spríngs;
the áutumn rain cóvers it with póols.
[8] They wálk with éver-growing stréngth;
the God of góds will appéar in Zíon.

[9] O LÓRD, God of hósts, hear my práyer;
give éar, O Gód of Jácob.
[10] Behóld our shíeld, O Gód;
lóok on the fáce of your anóinted.

[11] One dáy withín your cóurts
is bétter than a thóusand élsewhere.
The thréshold of the hóuse of my Gód
I prefér to the ténts of the wícked.

[12] For the LORD Gód is a sún, a shíeld;
the LORD will gíve us fávor and glóry,
And will nót withhóld any góod
from thóse who wálk without bláme.
[13] O LÓRD of hósts, how bléssed
is the óne who trústs in yóu!

Psalm 85 *(84)*

1 *For the Choirmaster. Of the sons of Korah. A Psalm.*

2 O LÓRD, you have fávored your lánd,
and brought báck the cáptives of Jácob.
3 You forgáve the guílt of your péople,
and cóvered áll their síns.
4 You avérted áll your ráge;
you túrned back the héat of your ánger.

5 Bring us báck, O Gód, our sávior!
Put an énd to your gríevance agáinst us.
6 Will you be ángry with ús forév er?
Will your ánger last from áge to áge?

7 Will you nót restóre again our lífe,
that your péople may rejóice in yóu?
8 Shów us, O LÓRD, your mércy,
and gránt us yóur salvátion.

9 I will héar what the LÓRD God spéaks,
who speaks of péace to his fáithful péople,
and those who túrn to Gód in their héarts.
10 For thóse who fear Gód, salvátion is néar,
and the Lord's glóry will dwéll in our lánd.

[11] Merciful lóve and fáithfulness have mét;
ríghteousness and péace have kíssed.
[12] Fáithfulness shall spríng from the éarth,
and ríghteousness look dówn from héaven.

[13] Also the Lórd will bestów a great bóunty,
and our éarth shall yíeld its íncrease.
[14] Ríghteousness will márch as a vánguard,
and gúide God's stéps on the wáy.

Psalm 86 *(85)*

[1] *A Prayer of David.*

Turn your éar, O Lórd, and ánswer me,
for Í am póor and néedy.
[2] Presérve my sóul, for I am fáithful;
save the sérvant who trústs in you, my Gód.

[3] Have mércy on mé, O Lórd,
for I crý to you áll the day lóng.
[4] Gládden the sóul of your sérvant,
for I líft up my sóul to you, O Lórd.

[5] O Lórd, you are góod and forgíving,
full of mércy to áll who call to yóu.
[6] Give éar, O Lórd, to my práyer,
and atténd to my vóice in supplicátion.

[7] In the dáy of distréss, I will cáll to you,
and súrely yóu will ánswer me.
[8] Among the góds there is nóne like you, O Lórd,
nor wórks to compáre with yóurs.

[9] All the nátions you have máde shall cóme;
they will bow dówn befóre you, O Lórd,
and glórify your náme,
[10] for you are gréat and do márvelous déeds,
yóu who alóne are Gód.

[11] Téach me, O LÓRD, your wáy,
so that Í may wálk in your trúth,
single-héartedly revéring your náme.

[12] I will práise you, Lord my Gód, with all my
héart,
and glórify your náme foréver.
[13] Your faithful lóve to mé has been gréat;
you have sáved me from the dépths of Shéol.

[14] The proud have rísen agáinst me, O Gód;
a bánd of the rúthless seeks my lífe.
To yóu they páy no héed.

[15] But you, O Gód, are compássionate and
grácious,
slów to ánger, O Lórd,
abúndant in lóve and fidélity;
[16] túrn and take píty on mé.

O gíve your stréngth to your sérvant,
and sáve the chíld of your hándmaid.
[17] Shów me the sígn of your fávor,
that my fóes may sée to their sháme
that you, O LÓRD, give me cómfort and hélp.

Psalm 87 (86)

[1] *Of the sons of Korah. A Psalm. A Song.*

Founded by Gód on the hóly móuntain,
[2] the Lórd loves the gátes of Zíon,
more than áll the dwéllings of Jácob.
[3] Of yóu are told glórious thíngs,
yóu, O cíty of Gód!

[4] "Rahab and Bábylon Í will cóunt
among thóse who knów me;
Of Tyre, Philístia, Ethiópia, it is tóld,
'Thére was thís one bórn.'
[5] But of Zíon it sháll be sáid,
'Each óne was bórn in hér.'"

Gód, the Most Hígh, will estáblish her.
[6] In the régister of péoples the Lord wrítes,
"Hére was thís one bórn."
[7] The síngers cry óut in chórus,
"Áll my wéllsprings are in yóu."

Psalm 88 *(87)*

[1] *A Song. A Psalm. Of the sons of Korah. For the Choirmaster. Intoned like* Mahalat Leannoth. *A* Maskil. *For Heman the Ezrahite.*

[2] O Lórd and Gód of my salvátion,
I crý before you dáy and níght.
[3] Let my práyer come fórth to your présence.
Inclíne your éar to my crý.
[4] For my sóul is fílled with évils;
my lífe is on the brínk of Shéol.

[5] I am réckoned as óne who goes dówn to the pít;
Í am like a wárrior without stréngth,
[6] like one róaming amóng the déad,
like the sláin who líe in the gráve,
like thóse you remémber no móre,
cut óff, as they áre, from your hánd.

[7] You have láid me in the dépths of the pít,
in régions that are dárk and déep.
[8] Your ánger wéighs down upón me;
I am drówned benéath your wáves.
[9] You have táken awáy my fríends;
to thém you have máde me háteful.

Imprísoned, I cannót escápe;
[10] my éyes are súnken with gríef.
I cáll to you, LÓRD, all day lóng;
to yóu I strétch out my hánds.

[11] Will you wórk your wónders for the déad?
Will the shádes rise úp to práise you?
[12] From the gráve, who can téll of your lóve?
From the pláce of perdítion your fáithfulness?
[13] Will your wónders be knówn in the dárk,
in the lánd of oblívion your ríghteousness?

[14] But Í, O LORD, crý out to yóu;
in the mórning my práyer comes befóre you.
[15] Whý do you rejéct me, O LÓRD?
Why do you híde your fáce from mé?

[16] I am wrétched, close to déath from my yóuth.
I have bórne your tríals; I am númb.
[17] Your fúry has swept dówn upón me;
your térrors have útterly destróyed me.

[18] They surróund me all the dáy like a flóod;
togéther they close ín agáinst me.
[19] Friend and néighbor you have táken awáy:
my óne compánion is dárkness.

Psalm 89 *(88)*

[1] *A* Maskil. *For Ethan the Ezrahite.*

[2] I will síng of your fáithful lóve, O Lord, foréver;
through all áges my móuth will procláim your fidélity.
[3] I have decláred your faithful lóve is estáblished foréver;
your fidélity stands fírm as the héavens.

[4] "With my chósen one Í have made a cóvenant;
I have swórn to Dávid my sérvant:
[5] I will estáblish your descéndants foréver,
and sét up your thróne through all áges."

[6] The héavens práise your wónders, O Lórd,
your fidélity, tóo, in the assémbly of your hóly ones.
[7] For whó in the skíes can compáre with the Lórd,
or whó is like the Lórd among the héavenly pówers?
[8] A Gód to be féared in the cóuncil of the hóly ones,
gréat and áwesome above áll aróund him.

[9] O Lórd God of hósts, whó is your équal?
You are míghty, O Lórd, and fidélity surróunds you.
[10] It is yóu who rúle the ráging of the séa;
it is yóu who stíll the súrging of its wáves.
[11] It is yóu who crush Ráhab underfóot like a córpse;
you scátter your fóes with your míghty árm.

[12] The héavens are yóurs, the éarth is yóurs;
yóu have fóunded the wórld and its fúllness;
[13] it is yóu who creáted the Nórth and the Sóuth.
Tábor and Hérmon shout for jóy at your náme.

[14] Yóurs is a míghty árm.
Your hánd is stróng; your right hánd is exálted.
[15] Ríghteousness and jústice are the píllars of your thróne;
loving kíndness and fidélity wálk in your présence.

[16] How bléssed the péople who knów your práise,
who wálk, O Lórd, in the líght of your fáce,
[17] who fínd their jóy every dáy in your náme,
who máke your ríghteousness their jóyful accláim.

[18] For yóu are the glóry of their stréngth;
by your fávor it ís that our míght is exálted;
[19] Behóld, the Lórd is our shíeld,
the Hóly One of Ísrael, our kíng.

[20] Thén you spóke in a vísion.
To your fáithful ónes you sáid,
"I have bestówed my hélp on a wárrior,
I have exálted one chósen from the péople.

[21] "I have fóund my sérvant Dávid,
and with my hóly óil anóinted him.
[22] My hánd shall álways be with hím,
and my árm shall máke him stróng.

[23] "The énemy shall néver outwít him,
nor shall the són of iníquity húmble him.
[24] I will béat down his fóes befóre him,
and thóse who háte him I will stríke.

[25] "My lóve and my fáithfulness shall bé with hím;
by my náme his míght shall bé exálted.
[26] I will strétch out his hánd to the Séa,
and his right hánd upón the Rívers.

[27] "He will call óut to me, 'Yóu are my fáther,
my Gód, the róck of my salvátion.'
[28] I for my párt will máke him my fírstborn,
the híghest of the kíngs of the éarth.

[29] "I will kéep my faithful lóve for him álways;
with hím my cóvenant shall lást.
[30] I will estáblish his descéndants forév er,
and his thróne as lásting as the dáys of héaven.

[31] "If his descéndants forsáke my láw
and refúse to wálk as I decrée,
[32] and if éver they víolate my státutes,
fáiling to kéep my commánds:

[33] "Then I will púnish their offénses with the ród;
then I will scóurge them on accóunt of their
guílt.
[34] But I will néver take báck my lóve;
my fidélity will néver fáil.
[35] I will néver víolate my cóvenant,
nor go báck on the prómise of my líps.

[36] "Once for áll, I have swórn by my hóliness.
'I will néver líe to Dávid.
[37] His descéndants shall contínue forévér.
In my síght his thróne is like the sún;
[38] like the móon, it shall endúre forévér,
a fáithful wítness in the héavens.'"

[39] But yet yóu have spúrned and rejécted,
you are ángry with the óne you have anóinted.
[40] You have renóunced your cóvenant with your
sérvant,
and dishónored his crówn in the dúst.

[41] You have bróken down áll his wálls,
and redúced his fórtresses to rúins.
[42] Áll who pass bý despóil him;
he has becóme the táunt of his néighbors.

[43] You have exálted the right hánd of his fóes;
you have máde all his énemies rejóice.
[44] You have turned báck the édge of his swórd;
you have nót uphéld him in báttle.

[45] You have bróught his glóry to an énd;
you have húrled his thróne to the gróund.
[46] You have cut shórt the dáys of his yóuth;
you have héaped disgráce upon hím.

[47] How lóng, O Lórd? Will you híde yourself forévér?
How lóng will your ánger búrn like a fíre?
[48] Remémber the shórtness of my lífe,
and how fráil you have máde the human ráce.
[49] Whó can líve and néver see déath?
Who can sáve themsélves from the grásp of Shéol?

[50] Where are your mércies of the pást, O Lórd,
which you swóre in your fáithfulness to Dávid?
[51] Remémber, O Lórd, the táunts to your sérvant,
how I béar in my bréast the scórn of many péoples.
[52] Thus your énemies líft up a táunt, O Lórd,
táunting your anóinted at évery stép.

* * *

[53] Blést be the Lórd forévér.
Amén and amén!

BOOK FOUR OF THE PSALTER

Psalm 90 (89)

[1] *Prayer of Moses, the man of God.*

O Lórd, yóu have been our réfuge,
from generátion tó generátion.
[2] Befóre the móuntains were bórn,
or the éarth or the wórld were brought fórth,
you are Gód, from áge to áge.

[3] You túrn human béings back to dúst,
and say, "Retúrn, O chíldren of Ádam."
[4] To your éyes a thóusand yéars
are like yésterday, cóme and góne,
or líke a wátch in the níght.

[5] You swéep them awáy like a dréam,
like gráss which is frésh in the mórning.
[6] In the mórning it spróuts and is frésh;
by évening it wíthers and fádes.

[7] Indéed, we are consúmed by your ánger;
we are strúck with térror at your fúry.
[8] You have sét our guílt befóre you,
our secret síns in the líght of your fáce.

[9] All our dáys pass awáy in your ánger.
Our yéars are consúmed like a sígh.
[10] Seventy yéars is the spán of our dáys,
or éighty if wé are stróng.
And móst of these are tóil and páin.
They pass swíftly and wé are góne.

[11] Who understánds the pówer of your ánger?
Your fúry mátches the féar of you.
[12] Then téach us to númber our dáys,
that wé may gain wísdom of héart.

[13] Turn báck, O Lórd! How lóng?
Show píty to your sérvants.
[14] At dawn, fíll us with your fáithful lóve;
we shall exúlt and rejóice all our dáys.
[15] Give us jóy for the dáys of our afflíction,
for the yéars when we lóoked upon évil.

[16] Let your déed be séen by your sérvants,
and your glórious pówer by their chíldren.
[17] Let the fávor of the Lórd our Gód be upón us;
give succéss to the wórk of our hánds.
O give succéss to the wórk of our hánds.

Psalm 91 (90)

[1] You who dwéll in the Most Hígh's hidden pláce,
and abíde in the sháde of the Almíghty,
[2] sáy to the Lórd, "My réfuge,
my strónghold, my Gód in whom I trúst!"

[3] The Lord will frée you from the snáre of the
fówler,
from the destrúctive plágue.
[4] The pínions of Gód will concéal you,
under wíngs of the Lórd you will find réfuge.
God's fáithfulness is búckler and shíeld.

[5] You will not féar the térror of the níght,
nor the árrow that flíes by dáy,
[6] nor the plágue that prówls in the dárkness,
nor the scóurge that lays wáste at nóon.

[7] A thóusand may fáll at your síde,
ten thóusand fáll at your ríght:
yóu it will néver appróach.

[8] Your éyes have ónly to lóok
to sée how the wícked are repáid.
[9] For yóu, O Lórd, are my réfuge.
You have máde the Most Hígh your dwélling.

[10] Upon yóu no évil shall fáll,
no plágue appróach your tént.
[11] For yóu has God commánded the ángels
to kéep you in áll your wáys.

[12] They shall béar you upón their hánds,
lest you stríke your fóot against a stóne.
[13] On the líon and the víper you will tréad,
and trámple the young líon and the sérpent.

[14] Since you clíng to me in lóve, I will frée you,
protéct you, for you knów my náme.
[15] When you cáll on mé, I will ánswer you;
I will bé with yóu in distréss;
I will delíver you, and gíve you glóry.

[16] With léngth of dáys I will contént you;
I will shów you my sáving pówer.

Psalm 92 *(91)*

[1] *A Psalm. A Song for the Sabbath.*

[2] It is góod to give thánks to the LÓRD,
to make músic to your náme, O Most Hígh,
[3] to procláim your faithful lóve in the mórning,
and your trúth in the wátches of the níght,
[4] on the tén-stringed lúte and the hárp,
with the sóund of sóng on the lýre.

[5] You have gláddened me, O LÓRD, by your déeds;
for the wórk of your hánds I shout with jóy.
[6] O LÓRD, how gréat are your wórks!
How déep are yóur desígns!
[7] The sénseless cánnot knów this,
and the fóol cannót understánd.

[8] Though the wícked spring úp like gráss,
and áll who do évil thríve,
they are dóomed to be etérnally destróyed.
[9] But you, O LÓRD, are etérnally on hígh.

[10] Sée, your énemies, O LÓRD,
sée, your énemies will pérish;
áll who do évil will be scáttered.

[11] You gíve me the stréngth of a wild óx;
you have poured óut on me púrest óil.
[12] My éyes looked in tríumph on my fóes;
my éars have héard of their fáll.

[13] The ríghteous will flóurish like the pálm tree,
and grów like a Lébanon cédar.

[14] Plánted in the hóuse of the LÓRD,
they will flóurish in the cóurts of our Gód,
[15] stíll bearing frúit when they are óld,
stíll full of sáp, still gréen,
[16] to procláim that the LÓRD is úpright.
In Gód, my róck, there is no wróng.

Psalm 93 *(92)*

[1] The LORD is kíng, with májesty enróbed.
The LÓRD is róbed with míght,
and gírded round abóut with pówer.

The wórld you made fírm, not to be móved;
[2] your thróne has stood fírm from of óld.
From all etérnity, O LÓRD, you áre.

[3] The flóods have lífted up, O LÓRD,
the flóods have lífted up their vóice;
the flóods have lífted up their thúnder.

[4] Gréater than the róar of mighty wáters,
míghtier than the súrgings of the séa,
the LÓRD is míghty on hígh.

[5] Trúly your decrées are to be trústed.
Hóliness is fítting to your hóuse,
O LÓRD, until the énd of tíme.

Psalm 94 (93)

[1] O Lórd, avénging Gód,
avénging Gód, shine fórth!
[2] Júdge of the éarth, aríse;
gíve the próud what they desérve!

[3] How lóng, O Lórd, shall the wícked,
how lóng shall the wícked tríumph?
[4] They blúster with árrogant spéech;
those who do évil bóast to each óther.

[5] They crúsh your péople, Lórd;
and they húmble yóur inhéritance.
[6] They kíll the wídow and the stránger,
and múrder the órphaned chíld.

[7] And they sáy, "The Lórd does not sée;
the God of Jácob páys no héed."
[8] Mark thís, you sénseless péople;
fóols, when wíll you understánd?

[9] Can the Óne who plánted the éar not héar?
Can the Óne who fórmed the éye not sée?
[10] Will the Óne who tráins the nátions not púnish?
Will the Óne who téaches us nót have knówledge?
[11] The Lórd knows the pláns of human béings,
knóws they are no móre than a bréath.

[12] Blessed are théy whom you díscipline, O Lórd,
whom you tráin by méans of your láw;
[13] to whóm you give péace in evil dáys,
while the pít is being dúg for the wícked.

[14] The Lórd will not forsáke the chosen péople,
nor abándon those who áre God's inhéritance;
[15] for júdgment shall agáin be ríghteous,
and all úpright héarts shall uphóld it.

[16] Who will stand úp for mé against the wícked?
Who will defénd me from thóse who do évil?
[17] If the Lórd were nót to hélp me,
my soul would sóon go dówn to the sílence.

[18] When I thínk, "I have lóst my fóothold,"
your faithful lóve, O Lórd, uphólds me.
[19] When cáres incréase in my héart,
your consolátion cálms my sóul.

[20] Can júdges who do évil be your fríends?
They do injústice under cóver of láw;
[21] they attáck the lífe of the ríghteous,
and condémn the ínnocent to déath.

[22] As for mé, the Lórd will be a strónghold;
my Gód will be the róck where I take réfuge.
[23] Gód will repáy them for their wíckedness,
destróy them for their évil déeds.
The Lórd, our Gód, will destróy them.

Psalm 95 (94)

1 Come, let us ríng out our jóy to the LÓRD;
hail the róck who sáves us.
2 Let us cóme before Gód giving thánks;
with songs of práise, let us háil the Lórd.

3 A míghty Gód is the LÓRD,
a great kíng abóve all góds,
4 in whose hánd are the dépths of the éarth,
and the héights of the móuntains as wéll.
5 The séa belongs to Gód, who máde it,
whose hánd shaped the drý land as wéll.

6 O cóme; let us bów and bend lów.
Let us knéel before the LÓRD who máde us,
7 for the Lórd is our Gód, and wé
the péople of the héavenly pásture,
the flock léd by the almíghty hánd.

O that todáy you would héed God's vóice!
[8] "Hárden not your héarts as at Méribah,
as on that dáy at Mássah in the désert
[9] when your áncestors pút me to the tést;
when they tríed me, though they sáw my wórk.

[10] "For forty yéars I abhórred that generátion,
and I sáid, 'Their héart goes astráy;
this péople does not knów my wáys.'
[11] Thén I took an óath in my ánger,
'Néver shall they énter my rést.'"

Psalm 96 (95)

[1] O síng a new sóng to the Lórd;
síng to the Lórd, all the éarth.
[2] O síng to the Lórd; bless God's náme.
Procláim divine salvátion day by dáy.
[3] Téll among the nátions God's glóry,
divine wónders amóng all the péoples.

[4] For the Lórd is great and híghly to be práised,
to be féared abóve all góds.
[5] For the ídols of the nátions are náught.
It was the Lórd who máde the héavens.
[6] Greatness and spléndor abóund in God's présence,
stréngth and hónor in the hóly place.

[7] Ascríbe to the Lórd, you fámilies of péoples,
Ascríbe to the Lórd glóry and pówer;
[8] Ascríbe to the Lórd the glóry of God's náme.

Bring an óffering and énter God's cóurts;
[9] wórship the Lórd in holy spléndor.
O trémble before Gód, all the éarth.

[10] Say to the nátions, "The Lórd is kíng,"
who made fírm the wórld in its pláce,
and who will júdge the péoples in fáirness.

[11] Let the héavens rejóice and earth be glád;
let the séa and all withín it thunder práise.
[12] Let the fíeld and all it béars rejóice.

Then all the trées of the wóod will shout for jóy
[13] at the présence of the Lórd who cómes;
God cómes to júdge the éarth.
The Lord will júdge the wórld with ríghteousness,
and the péoples with fáithfulness.

Psalm 97 (96)

[1] The LORD réigns, let éarth rejóice;
let the mány íslands be glád.
[2] Cloud and dárkness surróund the Lórd,
whose throne is fóunded on jústice and ríght.

[3] A fíre prepares the páthway of Gód;
it burns úp the Lord's fóes on every síde.
[4] God's líghtnings líght up the wórld;
while the éarth looks ón and trémbles.

[5] The móuntains mélt like wáx
befóre the fáce of the LÓRD,
before the fáce of the Lórd of all the éarth.
[6] The skíes procláim divine ríghteousness;
all péoples see the glóry of Gód.

[7] Let thóse who serve ídols be ashámed,
those who bóast of their wórthless góds.
All you ángels, wórship the Lórd.

[8] Zíon héars and is glád;
the cíties of Júdah rejóice
becáuse of your júdgments, O LÓRD.

[9] For yóu indéed are the LÓRD
most hígh above áll the éarth,
exálted fár above all góds.

[10] The LÓRD loves thóse who hate évil,
guárds the sóuls of the fáithful,
and séts them frée from the wícked.

[11] Líght shines fórth for the ríghteous,
and jóy for the úpright of héart.
[12] Rejóice in the LÓRD, you ríghteous;
in mémory of God's hóliness give thánks.

Psalm 98 *(97)*

[1] *A Psalm.*

O síng a new sóng to the LÓRD,
who has wórked such wónders,
whose right hánd and hóly árm
have bróught salvátion.

[2] The LÓRD has made knówn salvátion,
has shówn delíverance to the nátions.
[3] God has remémbered fáithful lóve
and trúth for the hóuse of Ísrael.

All the énds of the éarth have séen
the salvátion of our Gód.
[4] Shóut to the LÓRD, all the éarth;
break fórth into jóyous sóng,
and síng out your práise.

[5] Sing psálms to the Lórd with the hárp,
with the hárp and the sóund of sóng.
[6] With trúmpets and the sóund of the hórn,
raise a shóut before the Kíng, the Lórd.

[7] Let the séa and all withín it thúnder;
the wórld, and thóse who dwéll in it.
[8] Let the rívers cláp their hánds,
and the hílls ring out their jóy
[9] at the présence of the Lórd who cómes,
who comes to júdge the éarth.
The Lord will júdge the wórld with ríghteousness,
and the péoples with fáirness.

Psalm 99 (98)

[1] The LORD is kíng; the péoples trémble.
God is enthróned on the chérubim; earth quákes.
[2] The LÓRD is gréat in Zíon,
exálted over áll the péoples.

[3] Let them práise your gréat and awesome náme,
for the Lórd our Gód is hóly!
[4] O mighty Rúler, lóver of jústice,
you have estáblished whát is úpright;
you have made jústice and ríght in Jácob.

[5] Exált the LÓRD our Gód;
bow dówn befóre God's fóotstool,
for the Lórd our Gód is hóly!

[6] Amóng God's príests were Áaron and Móses;
among thóse who invóked God's náme was Sámuel.
They cried óut to the LÓRD, who ánswered.

[7] To thém the Lord spóke in the píllar of clóud.
They obéyed the decrées and the státutes
which the Lórd had gíven thém.

[8] O LÓRD our Gód, you ánswered them.
For thém you were a Gód who forgíves,
and yét you púnished their offénses.

[9] Exált the LÓRD our Gód;
bow dówn before the hóly móuntain,
for the LÓRD our Gód is hóly.

Psalm 100 (99)

[1] *A Psalm of Thanksgiving.*

Cry out with jóy to the LÓRD, all the éarth.
[2] Sérve the LÓRD with gládness.
Come befóre God, sínging for jóy.

[3] Knów that the LÓRD is Gód,
who máde us, to whóm we belóng.
We are God's péople, the shéep of God's flóck.

[4] Enter the témple gátes with thanksgíving
and its cóurts with sóngs of práise.
Give thánks and bléss God's náme.

[5] Indéed, how góod is the LÓRD,
etérnal God's mérciful lóve.
God is fáithful from áge to áge.

Psalm 101 (100)

[1] *Of David. A Psalm.*

I sing of fáithful lóve and jústice;
I raise a psálm to yóu, O LÓRD.
[2] I will pónder the wáy of the blámeless.
O whén will you cóme to mé?

I will wálk with blámeless héart
within my hóuse;
[3] I will not sét befóre my éyes
whatéver is báse.

I háte the déeds of the cróoked;
such I wíll not endúre.
[4] The false-héarted must kéep far awáy;
I wíll knów no évil.

[5] The one who slánders a néighbor in sécret
I will bríng to sílence.
Proud éyes and háughty héart
I will néver endúre.

[6] My éyes are on the fáithful of the lánd,
that they may dwéll with mé.
The one who wálks in the wáy of the blámeless
shall bé my sérvant.

[7] Nó one who práctices decéit
shall líve within my hóuse.
Nó one who útters líes
shall stánd before my éyes.

[8] Morning by mórning Í will subdúe
all the wícked in the lánd,
upróoting from the cíty of the Lórd
áll who do évil.

Psalm 102 *(101)*

[1] *Prayer of someone afflicted who is weary and pours out his trouble to the* L*ORD*.

[2] Héar my práyer, O Lórd,
and let my crý come to yóu.
[3] Do not híde your fáce from mé
in the dáy of my distréss.
Túrn your éar towards mé;
on the dáy when I cáll,
spéedily ánswer me.

[4] For my dáys are vánishing like smóke;
my bónes burn awáy like a fúrnace.
[5] My heart is wíthered and dried úp like the gráss.
I forgét to éat my bréad.
[6] Becáuse of the sóund of my gróaning,
my bónes hold fást to my flésh.

[7] I have becóme like a vúlture in the désert,
like an ówl amóng the rúins.
[8] I líe awáke and I móan,
like a bírd alóne on a róof.
[9] All day lóng my fóes revíle me;
those who deríde me use my náme as a cúrse.

[10] I have éaten áshes like bréad,
and míngled téars with my drínk.
[11] Becáuse of your ánger and fúry,
you have lífted me úp and thrown me dówn.
[12] My dáys are like a fáding shádow,
and I wíther awáy like the gráss.

[13] But you, O Lórd, are enthróned forévér,
and your renówn is from áge to áge.

[14] You will aríse and take píty on Zíon,
for thís is the tíme to have mércy;
yes, the tíme appóinted has cóme.
[15] Behold, your sérvants lóve her very stónes,
are móved to píty for her dúst.

[16] The nátions shall féar the náme of the Lórd,
and áll the earth's kíngs your glóry,
[17] when the Lórd shall buíld up Zíon,
and appéar in áll divine glóry.
[18] God will túrn to the práyers of the hélpless;
and will nót despíse their práyers.

[19] Let this be wrítten for áges to cóme,
that a péople yet unbórn may praise the Lórd;
[20] The Lord looked dówn from the hóly place on
high,
looked dówn from héaven to the éarth,
[21] to héar the gróans of the prísoners,
and frée those condémned to díe.

[22] May the náme of the Lórd be procláimed in
Zíon,
and práised in Jerúsalem,
[23] when péoples and kíngdoms are gáthered as óne
to óffer their wórship to the Lórd.

[24] The Lord has bróken my stréngth in midcóurse,
and has shórtened my dáys.
[25] I say: "My Gód, do not táke me awáy
before hálf of my dáys are compléte,
you, whose dáys last from áge to áge.

[26] Long agó you fóunded the éarth,
and the héavens are the wórk of your hánds.
[27] They will pérish but yóu will remáin.
They will áll wear óut like a gárment.
You will chánge them like clóthes, and they
chánge.
[28] But yóu are the sáme, and your yéars do not
énd."

[29] The chíldren of your sérvants shall dwéll
untróubled,
and their descéndants estáblished befóre you.

Psalm 103 *(102)*

[1] *Of David.*

Bléss the Lórd, O my sóul,
and all withín me, the hóly name of Gód.
[2] Bléss the Lórd, O my sóul,
and néver forgét all God's bénefits.

[3] It is the Lórd who forgíves all your síns,
who héals every óne of your ílls,
[4] who redéems your lífe from the gráve,
who crówns you with lóve and compássion,
[5] who fílls your lífe with good thíngs,
renéwing your yóuth like an éagle's.

[6] The Lórd does ríghteous déeds,
gives full jústice to áll who are oppréssed.
[7] The Lord made knówn divine wáys to Móses,
and wondrous déeds to the chíldren of Ísrael.

[8] The Lórd is compássionate and grácious,
slow to ánger and abóunding in lóve,
[9] not álways fínding fáult,
nor persísting in ánger foréver.
[10] God does not tréat us accórding to our síns,
nor repáy us accórding to our fáults.

[11] For as the héavens are hígh above the éarth,
so strong the mércy for thóse who fear Gód.
[12] As fár as the éast is from the wést,
so far from ús does God remóve our
transgréssions.

[13] As a fáther has compássion on his chíldren,
divine compássion is on thóse who féar the Lórd,
[14] who knóws of whát we are máde,
who remémbers that wé are dúst.

[15] Human béings, their dáys are like gráss;
they flówer like the flówer of the fíeld.
[16] The wind blóws, and it ís no móre,
and its pláce never sées it agáin.

[17] But the lóve of the Lórd is everlásting
upon thóse who revére godly wáys,
upon chíldren's chíldren divine ríghteousness
[18] for thóse who kéep the cóvenant,
and remémber to fulfíll its commánds.

[19] The Lord has fíxed a thróne in héaven,
and God's kíngdom is rúling over áll.
[20] Bless the Lórd, all you ángels of héaven,
mighty in pówer, fulfílling God's wórd,
who héed the vóice of God's wórd.

[21] Bléss the Lórd, all you hósts,
you sérvants, who dó God's wíll.
[22] Bléss the Lórd, all you créatures,
in évery pláce of God's domáin.
Bléss the Lórd, O my sóul!

Psalm 104 (103)

[1] Bléss the Lórd, O my sóul!
O Lord my Gód, how gréat you áre,
clóthed in májesty and hónor,
[2] wrápped in líght as with a róbe!

You strétch out the héavens like a tént;
[3] you lay béams on the wáters for your dwélling.
You máke the clóuds your cháriot;
you ríde on the wíngs of the wínd.
[4] You máke the wínds your méssengers,
fláme and fíre your sérvants.

[5] You sét the éarth on its foundátion,
immóvable from áge to áge.
[6] You wrápped it with the dépths like a clóak;
the wáters stood hígher than the móuntains.
[7] At your thréat they tóok to flíght;
at the vóice of your thúnder they fléd.

[8] The mountains róse, the válleys descénded
to the pláce which yóu had appóinted them.
[9] You set límits they míght not páss,
lest the dépths return to cóver the éarth.

[10] You make spríngs gush fórth in the válleys;
they flów in betwéen the hílls.
[11] They give drínk to all the béasts of the fíeld;
the wild ásses quénch their thírst.
[12] There the bírds of héaven build their nésts;
from the bránches they síng their sóng.

[13] From your dwélling you wáter the móuntains;
by your wórks the éarth has its fíll.

[14] You máke the grass grów for the cáttle
and plánts to sérve human néeds,
to bríng forth bréad from the éarth,
[15] and wíne to chéer people's héarts;
óil, to máke faces shíne,
and bread to stréngthen the húman héart.

[16] The trées of the LÓRD drink their fíll,
and the cédars plánted on Lébanon;
[17] thére the bírds build their nésts;
on the tréetop the stórk has a hóme.
[18] For the góats the lófty móuntains,
for the rábbits the rócks are a réfuge.

[19] You made the móon to márk the mónths;
the sún knows the tíme for its sétting.
[20] You spréad the dárkness, it is níght,
and all the béasts of the fórest creep fórth.
[21] The young líons róar for their préy,
and séek their fóod from Gód.

[22] At the rísing of the sún they steal awáy;
and they gó to lie dówn in their déns.
[23] Péople go fórth to their wórk,
to lábor till évening fálls.

[24] How mány are your wórks, O Lórd!
In wísdom you have máde them áll.
The éarth is fúll of your créatures.

[25] Vast and wíde is the spán of the séa,
with its créeping thíngs past cóunting,
líving things gréat and smáll.
[26] The shíps are móving thére,
and Levíathan you máde to pláy with.

[27] Áll of these lóok to yóu
to gíve them their fóod in due séason.
[28] You gíve it, they gáther it úp;
you ópen wide your hánd, they are well filled.

[29] You híde your fáce, they are dismáyed;
you táke away their bréath, they díe,
retúrning to the dúst from which they cáme.
[30] When you sénd forth your bréath, they are
créated,
and you renéw the fáce of the éarth.

[31] May the glóry of the LÓRD last foréver!
May the LÓRD rejóice in these wórks!
[32] God lóoks on the éarth and it trémbles;
tóuches the móuntains and they smóke.

[33] I will síng to the LÓRD all my lífe,
sing psálms to my Gód while I líve.
[34] May my thóughts be pléasing to Gód.
Í will rejóice in the LÓRD.

[35] Let sínners vánish from the éarth,
and the wícked exíst no móre.
Bléss the LÓRD, O my sóul.

Alleluia!

Psalm 105 *(104)*

[1] Give thánks and procláim the náme of the Lórd;
make knówn God's déeds among the péoples.

[2] O síng to Gód, sing práise;
tell all the wónderful wórks of the Lórd!
[3] Glóry in the hóly name of Gód;
let héarts that seek the Lórd rejóice.

[4] Túrn to the Lórd who is stróng;
cónstantly séek God's fáce.
[5] Remémber the wónders the Lórd has dóne,
great márvels and wórds of júdgment.

[6] O chíldren of Ábraham, God's sérvant,
O descéndants of Jácob the chósen one,
[7] it is the Lórd who ís our Gód,
whose júdgments are in áll the éarth.

[8] The Lord remémbers the cóvenant foréver:
the prómise ordáined for a thóusand generátions,
[9] the cóvenant máde with Ábraham,
the óath that was swórn to Ísaac.

[10] God confírmed it for Jácob as a láw,
for Ísrael as a cóvenant foréver:
[11] "I will gíve you the lánd of Cánaan
to bé your allótted inhéritance."

[12] When théy were féw in númber,
a hándful of strángers in the lánd,
[13] when they wándered from nátion to nátion,
from one kíngdom and péople to anóther,

[14] God allówed nó one to oppréss them;
and admónished kíngs on their accóunt,
[15] saying, "Thóse I have anóinted, do not tóuch;
do no hárm to ány of my próphets."

[16] But a fámine was cálled down on the lánd;
their stáff of bréad was bróken.
[17] God had sént a mán ahéad of them,
Jóseph, sóld as a sláve.

[18] His féet were wéighed down in cháins,
his néck was bóund with íron,
[19] untíl what God sáid came to páss,
and the wórd of the Lórd proved him trúe.

[20] Then the kíng sent órders and reléased him;
the rúler of the péoples set him frée.
[21] He máde him máster of his hóuse
and rúler of áll his posséssions,
[22] to instrúct his prínces from his héart,
and to téach his élders wísdom.

[23] So Ísrael cáme into Égypt;
Jacob sójourned in the lánd of Hám.
[24] The Lord gáve this péople great íncrease,
and máde them strónger than their fóes,
[25] whose héarts were turned to háte the Lord's
péople,
and to déal with decéit toward God's sérvants.

[26] Then Móses, God's sérvant, was sént,
and Áaron whom Gód had chósen.
[27] They perfórmed great sígns amóng them,
and wónders in the lánd of Hám.

[28] God sent dárkness, and dárkness cáme,
but they rebélled against the wórds of Gód;
[29] the Lord túrned their wáters into blóod,
and cáused their físh to díe.

[30] Their lánd was overrún by frógs,
éven to the hálls of their kíngs.
[31] God spóke; there came swárms of flíes,
and gnáts covered áll the cóuntry.

[32] In pláce of the ráin there came háilstones,
and líghtning fláshing in their lánd;
[33] God strúck their vínes and fíg trees,
and shattered the trées through their cóuntry.

[34] God spóke; the lócusts came fórth,
young lócusts, too mány to be cóunted.
[35] They áte up every plánt in the lánd;
they áte up all the frúit of their fíelds.

[36] All the fírstborn in their lánd were strúck,
the first frúit of áll their stréngth.
[37] God led out Ísrael with sílver and góld.
In the tríbes were nóne who stúmbled.

[38] Égypt rejóiced when they léft,
for dréad had fállen upón them.
[39] God spréad a clóud as a scréen,
and fíre to illúmine the níght.

[40] When they ásked, the Lord sént them quáils,
and fílled them with bréad from héaven.
[41] The rock was piérced and wáter gushed fórth;
in the désert it flówed as a ríver.

[42] For God remémbered the hóly wórd
spoken to Ábraham, sérvant of the Lórd,
[43] God bróught out the péople with jóy,
the chósen ones with shóuts of rejóicing.

[44] The Lord gáve them the lánds of the nátions.
They inhérited the frúits of the péoples' tóil,
[45] that thús they might kéep divine précepts,
that thús they might obsérve God's láws.

Alleluia!

Psalm 106 (105)

[1] Alleluia!

O give thánks to the Lórd, who is góod,
whose faithful lóve endúres forévér.
[2] Who can téll the Lórd's mighty déeds,
or recóunt God's práise in fúll?

[3] Blessed are théy who obsérve what is júst,
who at áll times dó what is ríghteous.
[4] O Lórd, remémber mé
with the fávor you shów to your péople.

Visit mé with your sáving pówer,
[5] that I may sée the ríches of your chósen ones,
and may rejóice in the gládness of your nátion,
bóasting in the glóry of your héritage.

[6] Like our fórebears, wé have sínned.
We have done wróng; our déeds have been évil.
[7] Our fórebears, when théy were in Égypt,
did not grásp the méaning of your wónders.

They forgót the great númber of your mércies,
at the Réd Sea they defíed the Most Hígh.
[8] Yet you sáved them for the sáke of your náme,
in órder to make knówn your pówer.

[9] You rebúked the Red Séa; it dried úp,
and you léd them through the déep as through
the désert.
[10] You sáved them from the hánd of the fóe;
and fréed them from the gríp of the énemy.

[11] The wáters cóvered their oppréssors;
not óne of thém was léft.
[12] Thén they belíeved in your wórds;
thén they sáng your práises.

[13] But they sóon forgót your déeds,
and wóuld not wáit upon your cóunsel.
[14] They yíelded to their crávings in the désert,
and put Gód to the tést in the wílderness.

[15] You gránted them the fávor they ásked,
but strúck them with a wásting diséase.
[16] In the cámp, they were jéalous of Móses,
and also Áaron, who was hóly to the Lórd.

[17] The earth ópened and swállowed up Dáthan,
and búried the clán of Abíram.
[18] Fíre blazed úp against their clán,
and flámes devóured the wícked.

[19] They fáshioned a cálf at Hóreb,
and wórshiped an ímage of métal;
[20] théy exchánged their glóry
for the ímage of a búll that eats gráss.

[21] They forgót the Gód who was their sávior,
who had dóne such gréat things in Égypt,
[22] such wónders in the lánd of Hám,
such áwesome déeds at the Red Séa.

[23] For thís God thréatened to destróy them,
but Móses, the mán God had chósen,
stóod in the bréach befóre them,
to túrn back God's ánger from destrúction.

[24] Then they scórned the desírable lánd;
they hád no fáith in your wórd.
[25] They compláined insíde their ténts,
and did not lísten to your vóice, O Lórd.

[26] So you ráised your hánd to them and swóre
that you would láy them lów in the désert,
[27] would dispérse their descéndants through the
nátions
and scátter them throughóut the lánds.

[28] They bówed before the Báal of Péor,
ate ófferings máde to what is lífeless.
[29] They róused you to ánger with their déeds,
and a plágue broke óut amóng them.

[30] Then Phínehas stood úp and intervénéd.
Thús the plágue was énded,
[31] and this was cóunted to hím as ríghteous
from áge to áge forévér.

[32] They provóked you at the wáters of Méribah.
Through their fáult it went íll with Móses,
[33] for they máde his spírit grow bítter,
and he úttered wórds that were rásh.

[34] They fáiled to destróy the péoples,
as you, O Lórd, had commánded thém;
[35] instéad they míngled with the nátions,
and léarned to áct as théy did.

[36] They álso sérved their ídols,
and thése became a snáre to entráp them.
[37] They éven óffered their sóns
and their dáughters in sácrifice to démons.

[38] They póured out ínnocent blóod,
the blóod of their sóns and dáughters,
whom they óffered to the ídols of Cánaan.
The lánd was pollúted with blóod.

[39] So they defíled themsélves by their áctions;
their déeds were thóse of a hárlot.
[40] Then your ánger blázed against your péople;
you were fílled with hórror at your héritage.

[41] So you hánded them óver to the nátions,
and their fóes becáme their rúlers.
[42] Their énemies álso oppréssed them;
they were subdúed benéath their hánd.

[43] Tíme after tíme you réscued them,
but in their málice they dáred to defý you,
and were wéakened even móre by their guílt.
[44] In spite of thís you paid héed to their distréss,
so óften as you héard their crý.

[45] For their sáke you remémbered your cóvenant.
In the gréatness of your lóve, you relénted,
[46] and lét them be tréated with compássion
by áll who héld them cáptive.

[47] Sáve us, O Lórd our Gód!
And gáther ús from the nátions,
to give thánks to your hóly náme,
and máke it our glóry to práise you.

* * *

[48] Blést be the Lórd, God of Ísrael,
foréver, from áge to áge.
Let áll the péople sáy,
"Amén! Amén! Allelúia!"

BOOK FIVE OF THE PSALTER

Psalm 107 (106)

[1] "O give thánks to the LÓRD who is góod,
whose faithful lóve endúres foréver."
[2] Let the redéemed of the LÓRD say thís,
those redéemed from the hánd of the fóe,
[3] and gáthered from fár-off lánds,
from éast and wést, north and sóuth.

[4] They wándered in a bárren désert,
finding no wáy to a cíty they could dwéll in.
[5] Húngry they wére and thírsty;
their sóul was fáinting withín them.

[6] Then they críed to the LÓRD in their néed,
and God réscued thém from their distréss,
[7] guíding them alóng a straight páth,
to réach a cíty they could dwéll in.

[8] Let them give thánks for the lóve of the LÓRD,
such wónders for the húman ráce:
[9] God sátisfies the thírsty sóul,
and fílls the húngry with good thíngs.

[10] Some dwelt in dárkness and the shádow of déath,
prísoners in mísery and cháins,
[11] having rebélled against the wórds of Gód,
and spúrned the plán of the Most Hígh.
[12] God húmbled their héart with tóil.
They stúmbled; there was nó one to hélp.

[13] Then they críed to the Lórd in their néed,
and God réscued thém from their distréss,
[14] leading them óut of dárkness and the shádow of
déath,
bréaking their cháins to píeces.

[15] Let them give thánks for the lóve of the Lórd,
God's wónders for the húman ráce:
[16] God búrsts the gátes of brónze,
and cúts through the íron bárs.

[17] Some fell síck on accóunt of their síns,
and were afflícted on accóunt of their guílt.
[18] They had a lóathing for évery fóod;
they drew néar to the gátes of déath.

[19] Then they críed to the Lórd in their néed,
and God réscued thém from their distréss,
[20] sénding forth a wórd to héal them,
sáving their lífe from destrúction.

[21] Let them give thánks for the lóve of the Lórd,
God's wónders for the húman ráce.
[22] Let them óffer a sácrifice of thánks,
and téll of God's déeds with rejóicing.

[23] Some went dówn to the séa in shíps,
to tráde on the míghty wáters.
[24] These have séen the déeds of the Lórd,
the wónders dóne in the déep.

[25] For the Lord spóke and ráised up the stórm-wind,
tóssing high the wáves of the séa
[26] that surged to héaven and drópped to the dépths.
Their souls mélted awáy in their distréss.

[27] They stággered and réeled like drúnkards,
for áll their skíll was góne.
[28] Then they críed to the Lórd in their néed,
and God réscued thém from their distréss.

[29] The Lord stílled the stórm to a whísper,
and the wáves of the séa were húshed.
[30] They rejóiced becáuse of the cálm,
and God léd them to the háven they desíred.

[31] Let them give thánks for the lóve of the Lórd,
God's wónders for the húman ráce.
[32] Let them exált God in the péople's assémbly,
praise the Lórd in the méeting of the élders.

[33] The Lord chánges rívers into désert,
springs of wáter into thírsty gróund,
[34] fruitful lánd into a sálty wáste,
for the wíckedness of thóse who líve there.

[35] God changes désert into póols of wáter,
thirsty gróund into spríngs of wáter.
[36] Thére the húngry are séttled,
and they estáblish a cíty to dwéll in.

[37] They sow fíelds and plánt their vínes,
which yíeld an abúndant hárvest.
[38] God blésses them; they grów in númbers,
God does nót let their cáttle decréase.

[39] Théy are dimínished and brought lów
by oppréssion, évil, and sórrow.
[40] The Lord póurs contémpt upon prínces,
makes them wánder in tráckless wástes.

[41] But God ráises the néedy from distréss;
makes fámilies númerous as a flóck.
[42] The úpright sée it and rejóice,
while all the wícked clóse their móuths.

[43] Whoever is wíse should héed these thíngs,
and understánd the loving mércy of the LÓRD.

Psalm 108 *(107)*

[1] *A Song. A Psalm of David.*

[2] My héart is réady, O Gód;
my héart is réady.
I will síng, I will síng your práise.
Awáke, my sóul;
[3] Awáke, O lýre and hárp.
I will awáke the dáwn.

[4] I will práise you, Lórd, among the péoples;
I will sing psálms to yóu among the nátions,
[5] for your fáithful love is hígher than the héavens,
and your trúth reaches the skíes.

[6] Be exálted, O Gód, above the héavens;
may your glóry shine on áll the éarth!
[7] With your right hánd, grant salvátion and give
ánswer;
O cóme and delíver your fríends.

[8] From his hóly place Gód has made this prómise:
"I will exúlt, and divíde the land of Shéchem;
I will méasure out the válley of Súccoth.

[9] Gílead is míne, as is Manásseh;
Éphraim I táke for my hélmet,
Júdah ís my scépter.
[10] Móab ís my wáshbowl;
on Édom I will tóss my shóe.
Over Philístia I will shóut in tríumph."

[11] But who will léad me to the fórtified cíty?
Whó will bríng me to Édom?
[12] Have you not cást us óff, O Gód?
Will you márch with our ármies no lónger?

[13] Give us aíd agáinst the fóe,
for húman hélp is váin.
[14] With Gód, wé shall do brávely;
the Lord will trámple dówn our fóes.

Psalm 109 *(108)*

[1] *For the Choirmaster. Of David. A Psalm.*

O Gód whom I práise, do not be sílent,
[2] for the móuths of decéit and wíckedness
are ópened agáinst me.

[3] They spéak to me with lýing tóngues;
they besét me with wórds of háte,
and attáck me without cáuse.

[4] In retúrn for my lóve, they accúse me,
while Í am at práyer for them.
[5] They repáy me évil for góod,
hátred for lóve.

* * *

[6] Appóint someone wícked as their júdge;
let an accúser stánd at their ríght.
[7] When júdged, let them cóme out condémned;
let their práyer be consídered as sín.

[8] Let the dáys of their líves be féw;
let anóther assúme their óffice.
[9] Let their chíldren be fátherless órphans,
and their wíves becóme wídows.

[10] Let their chíldren be wánderers and béggars,
dríven from the rúins of their hóme.
[11] Let the créditor séize all their góods;
let strángers take the frúit of their wórk.

[12] Let nó one shów them any mércy,
nor píty their fátherless chíldren.
[13] Let their postérity bé cut óff,
in a generátion their námes blotted óut.

[14] Let their fáthers' guílt be remémbered to the Lórd,
their móthers' síns be retáined.
[15] Let them álways stánd before the Lórd,
that their mémory be cut óff from the éarth.

[16] For théy did not thínk of showing mércy,
but pursúed the póor and the néedy,
hóunding to déath the brokenhéarted.
[17] They loved cúrsing; let cúrses fall on thém.
They scorned bléssing; let bléssing pass them bý.

[18] They pút on cúrsing like a cóat:
let it sínk into their bódies like wáter;
let it sínk like óil into their bónes.
[19] Let it bé like the clóthes that cóver them,
like bélts they wéar all the tíme.

[20] Let the Lórd thus repáy my accúsers,
all thóse who speak évil agáinst me.
[21] But yóu, O Lórd, my Lórd,
do with mé as befíts your náme.
How góod your faithful lóve! Delíver me.

[22] For Í am póor and néedy,
and my héart is píerced withín me.
[23] I fáde like an évening shádow;
I am sháken óff like a lócust.

[24] My knées are wéak from fásting;
my bódy is thín and gáunt.
[25] I have becóme an óbject of scórn;
when they sée me they sháke their héads.

[26] Hélp me, LÓRD my Gód;
sáve me with your fáithful lóve.
[27] Let them knów that thís is your hánd,
that thís is your dóing, O LÓRD.

[28] They may cúrse, but yóu will bléss.
Let my attáckers be pút to sháme,
but lét your sérvant rejóice.
[29] Let my accúsers be clóthed with dishónor,
cóvered with sháme as with a clóak.

[30] Loud thánks to the LÓRD are on my líps,
with práise in the mídst of the thróng,
[31] for the Lord stánds at the right hánd of the póor,
to sáve their souls from thóse who condémn
them.

Psalm 110 *(109)*

[1] *Of David. A Psalm.*

The LÓRD's revelátion to my lórd:
"Sít at my right hánd,
until I máke your fóes your fóotstool."

[2] The LÓRD will sénd from Zíon
your scépter of pówer:
rúle in the mídst of your fóes.

[3] With yóu is príncely rúle
on the dáy of your pówer.
In holy spléndor, from the wómb before the dáwn,
I have begótten yóu.

[4] The LÓRD has sworn an óath he will not chánge:
"Yóu are a príest forévér,
accórding to the órder of Melchízedek."

[5] The Lórd at yóur right hánd
shatters rúlers on the dáy of God's wráth.

[6] The Lórd brings a júdgment on the nátions,
and héaps the bódies hígh,
and shatters héads throughóut the wide éarth.

[7] He shall drínk from the stréam by the wáyside,
and thérefore he shall líft up his héad.

Psalm 111 (110)

[1] Alleluia!

I will thánk the Lórd with all my héart,
in the méeting of the júst and the assémbly.
[2] Gréat are the wórks of the Lórd,
to be póndered by áll who delíght in them.

[3] Majéstic and glórious your wórk;
your ríghteousness stands fírm foréver.
[4] You have máde a memórial of your wónders.
You, O Lórd, are grácious and mérciful.

[5] You give fóod to thóse who revére you;
you are míndful of your cóvenant foréver.
[6] You have shówn mighty wórks to your péople
by gíving them the héritage of nátions.

[7] Your hándiwork is jústice and trúth,
your précepts are áll of them súre,
[8] standing fírm foréver and éver,
wróught in úprightness and trúth.

[9] You have sént redémption to your péople,
and estáblished your cóvenant foréver.
Hóly your náme, to be féared.

[10] Fear of the Lórd is the begínning of wísdom;
understánding marks áll who live by ít.
Your práise endúres foréver!

Psalm 112 (111)

[1] Alleluia!

Bléssed are thóse who fear the LÓRD,
who táke great delíght in God's commánds.
[2] Their descéndants shall be pówerful on éarth;
the generátion of the úpright will be blést.

[3] Ríches and wéalth are in their hóuses;
their ríghteousness stands fírm forever.
[4] A light ríses in the dárkness for the úpright;
they are génerous, lóving and ríghteous.

[5] It goes wéll for thóse who deal génerously and
lénd,
who condúct their affáirs with jústice.
[6] Théy will néver be móved;
forever shall the ríghteous be remémbered.

[7] They háve no féar of evil néws;
with a firm héart, they trúst in the LÓRD.
[8] With stéadfast héarts they will not féar;
they will sée the dównfall of their fóes.

[9] Openhánded, they gíve to the póor;
their ríghteousness stands fírm forever.
Their míght shall be exálted in glóry.

[10] The wícked sée and are ángry,
grind their téeth and fáde awáy;
the desíre of the wícked leads to dóom.

Psalm 113 (*112*)

[1] Alleluia!

Práise, O sérvants of the Lórd,
práise the náme of the Lórd!
[2] May the náme of the Lórd be blést
both nów and forévermóre!
[3] From the rísing of the sún to its sétting,
práised be the náme of the Lórd!

[4] Hígh above all nátions is the Lórd,
above the héavens God's glóry.
[5] Whó is like the Lórd, our Gód,
who dwélls on hígh,
[6] who stóops from the héights to look dówn
upon héaven and éarth?

[7] From the dúst the Lord lífts up the lówly,
from the ásh heap ráises the póor,
[8] to sét them in the cómpany of léaders,
yés, with the léaders of the péople.
[9] To the chíldless wífe God gives a hóme
as a jóyful móther of chíldren.

Psalm 114 (113A)

[1] Alleluia!

When Ísrael came fórth from Égypt,
the house of Jácob from a fóreign péople,
[2] Júdah becáme God's hóly place,
Ísrael the Lórd's domáin.

[3] The séa behéld them and fléd;
the Jórdan turned báck on its cóurse.
[4] The móuntains léapt like ráms,
and the híllls like yéarling shéep.

[5] Whý was it, séa, that you fléd;
that you túrned back, Jórdan, on your cóurse?
[6] O móuntains, that you léapt like ráms;
O hílls, like yéarling shéep?

[7] Trémble, O éarth, before the Lórd,
in the présence of the Gód of Jácob,
[8] who túrns the róck into a póol,
and flínt into a spríng of wáter.

Psalm 115 (*113B*)

[1] Not to ús, O Lórd, not to ús,
but to your náme give glóry,
for your fáithful lóve and fidélity.
[2] Whý should the nátions sáy:
"Whére is their Gód?"

[3] But our Gód is ín the héavens,
and wílls whatéver should be dóne.
[4] Their ídols are sílver and góld,
the wórk of húman hánds.

[5] They have móuths but they cánnot spéak;
they have éyes but they cánnot sée.
[6] They have éars but they cánnot héar;
they have nóstrils but they cánnot sméll.

[7] They have hánds but they cánnot féel;
they have féet but they cánnot wálk.
They máke no sóund from their thróats.
[8] Their mákers will cóme to be líke them,
as will áll who trúst in thém.

[9] House of Ísrael, trúst in the Lórd:
their hélp and their shíeld is Gód.
[10] House of Áaron, trúst in the Lórd:
their hélp and their shíeld is Gód.
[11] You who féar the Lord, trúst in the Lórd:
your hélp and your shíeld is Gód.

[12] The Lord remémbers ús and will bléss us,
will bléss the hóuse of Ísrael.
God will bléss the hóuse of Áaron.

[13] Those who féar the Lórd will be blést,
the líttle no léss than the gréat.
[14] To yóu may the Lórd grant íncrease,
to yóu and áll your chíldren.

[15] Máy you be blést by the Lórd,
the máker of héaven and éarth.
[16] The héavens, the héavens belóng to the Lórd,
but to the húman ráce God has gíven the éarth.

[17] The déad shall not práise the Lórd,
nor thóse who go dówn into sílence.
[18] But wé who líve bless the Lórd
both nów and forévermóre.

Alleluia!

Psalm 116A *(114:1–9; 115)*

[1] I lóve the Lórd who has héard
my vóice, my appéal;
[2] For God has túrned an éar to mé
whenéver I cáll.

[3] They surróunded me, the snáres of déath;
the ánguish of Shéol has fóund me;
ánguish and sórrow I fóund.
[4] I cálled on the náme of the Lórd:
"Delíver my sóul, O Lórd!"

[5] How grácious is the Lórd, and ríghteous;
our Gód has compássion.
[6] The Lórd protécts the símple;
I was brought lów, and was sáved.

[7] Turn báck, my sóul, to your rést,
for the Lórd has been góod to yóu,
[8] God has képt my sóul from déath,
my eyes from téars, and my féet from stúmbling.
[9] I will wálk in the présence of the Lórd
in the lánd of the líving.

Psalm 116B *(115:10–19)*

[10] I trústed, éven when I sáid,
"I am sórely afflícted,"
[11] and whén I sáid in my alárm,
"All péople are untrúthful."

[12] Hów can I repáy the Lórd
for all the góodness shówn to mé?
[13] The cúp of salvátion I will ráise;
I will cáll on the náme of the Lórd.

[14] My vóws to the Lórd I will fulfíll
before áll the péople.
[15] How précious in the éyes of the Lórd
is the déath of God's fáithful.

[16] Your sérvant, Lord, your sérvant am Í,
you have lóosened my bónds.
[17] I will óffer you a thánksgiving sácrifice;
I will cáll on the náme of the Lórd.

[18] My vóws to the Lórd I will fulfíll
before áll the péople,
[19] in the cóurts of the hóuse of the Lórd,
in your mídst, O Jerúsalem.

Alleluia!

Psalm 117 (116)

[1] O práise the Lórd, all you nátions;
acclaím God, áll you péoples!

[2] For God's fáithful lóve toward us is gréat;
the Lórd remains fáithful forév er.

Alleluia!

Psalm 118 (117)

[1] Give thánks to the Lórd, who is góod,
whose faithful lóve endúres foréver.

[2] Let the hóuse of Ísrael sáy,
"God's faithful lóve endúres foréver."
[3] Let the hóuse of Áaron sáy,
"God's faithful lóve endúres foréver."
[4] Let thóse who féar the Lord sáy,
"God's faithful lóve endúres foréver."

[5] I cálled to the Lórd in my distréss;
the Lórd has ánswered and fréed me.
[6] The Lórd is at my síde; I do not féar.
What can ányone dó agáinst me?
[7] The Lórd is at my síde as my hélper;
I shall lóok in tríumph on my fóes.

[8] It is bétter to take réfuge in the Lórd
than to trúst in human béings;
[9] it is bétter to take réfuge in the Lórd
than to trúst in rúlers.

[10] The nátions all encírcled mé;
in the náme of the Lórd I cut them óff.
[11] They encírcled me áll aróund;
in the náme of the Lórd I cut them óff.

[12] They encírcled me abóut like bées;
they blázed like a fíre among thórns.
In the náme of the Lórd I cut them óff.

[13] They púshed me, pushed me hárd to knock me
dówn,
but the Lórd was my hélper.
[14] The Lórd is my stréngth and my sóng,
and has béen my sávior.

[15] There are shóuts of jóy and salvátion
in the ténts of the ríghteous.
"The Lord's right hánd has done míghty déeds;
[16] The Lórd's right hánd is exálted.
The Lord's right hánd has done míghty déeds."

[17] Í shall not díe, I shall líve
and recóunt the déeds of the Lórd.
[18] The Lórd has púnished me sevérely,
but did not hánd me óver to déath.

[19] Open to mé the gátes of ríghteousness:
I will énter and thánk the Lórd.
[20] Thís is the gáte of the Lórd,
where the júst may énter.
[21] I will thánk you, for yóu have ánswered,
and yóu are my sávior.

[22] The stóne that the buílders rejécted
has becóme the córnerstone.
[23] By the Lórd has thís been dóne,
a márvel in our éyes.
[24] This is the dáy the Lórd has máde;
let us rejóice in ít and be glád.

[25] We beséech you, O Lórd, grant salvátion;
We beséech you, O Lórd, grant succéss.
[26] Blést is hé who cómes
in the náme of the Lórd.
We bléss you from the hóuse of the Lórd;
[27] the Lord is Gód, and has gíven us líght.

Go fórward in procéssion with bránches,
as fár as the hórns of the áltar.
[28] Yóu are my Gód, I thánk you.
My Gód, I práise you.
[29] Give thánks to the Lórd, who is góod,
whose faithful lóve endúres foréver.

Psalm 119 *(118):**1–8***
Aleph

[1] Blessed are thóse whose wáy is blámeless,
who wálk in the láw of the Lórd!
[2] Blessed are thóse who kéep his decrées!
With áll their héarts they séek him.

[3] They néver do ánything évil,
but wálk in God's wáys.
[4] Yóu have láid down your précepts
to be cárefully képt.

[5] Máy my wáys be fírm
in kéeping your státutes.
[6] Thén I shall nót be put to sháme
as I fíx my eyes on áll your commánds.

[7] I will thánk you with an úpright héart,
as I léarn your righteous júdgments.
[8] Í will kéep your státutes;
do not éver forsáke me.

Psalm 119 (118):9–16
Beth

[9] How shall a yóuth remain púre on life's wáy?
By obéying your wórd.
[10] I séek you with áll my héart;
let me not stráy from your commánds.

[11] I tréasure your wórd in my héart,
lest I sín agáinst you.
[12] Blést are yóu, O Lórd;
téach me your státutes.

[13] With my líps have Í recóunted
all the decrées of your móuth.
[14] I rejóice in the wáy of your précepts,
as though all ríches were míne.

[15] Í will pónder your précepts,
and consíder your páths.
[16] I táke delíght in your státutes;
I will nót forget your wórd.

Psalm 119 *(118):**17–24***
Gimel

[17] Deal bóuntifully wíth your sérvant,
that I may líve and keep your wórd.
[18] Ópen my éyes, that I may sée
the wónders of your láw.

[19] Í am a pílgrim in the lánd;
híde not your commánds from mé.
[20] My sóul is consúmed with lónging
at all tímes for yóur decrées.

[21] You thréaten the próud, the accúrsed,
who stráy from your commánds.
[22] Frée me from scórn and contémpt,
for I obsérve your decrées.

[23] Though prínces sit plótting agáinst me,
your servant pónders your státutes.
[24] Sée, your decrées are my delíght;
your státutes are my cóunselors.

Psalm 119** (118)**:25–32
Daleth

[25] My sóul holds fást to the dúst;
revíve me by your wórd.
[26] I declåred my wáys and you ánswered me;
téach me your státutes.

[27] Make me grásp the wáy of your précepts,
and I will pónder your wónders.
[28] My sóul pines awáy with gríef;
by your wórd raise me úp.

[29] Kéep me from the wáy of fálsehood;
grant me mércy by your láw.
[30] I have chósen the wáy of fáithfulness;
your decrées I have uphéld.

[31] I clíng to your decrées, O Lórd;
let me nót be put to sháme.
[32] I will rún the wáy of your commánds;
you open wíde my héart.

Psalm 119** (118):**33–40
He

[33] Lord, téach me the wáy of your státutes,
and I will kéep them to the énd.
[34] Grant me ínsight that Í may keep your láw,
and obsérve it wholehéartedly.

[35] Guíde me in the páth of your commánds,
for in thém is my delíght.
[36] Bénd my héart to your decrées,
and not to wróngful gáin.

[37] Turn my éyes from gázing on vánities;
in your wáy, give me lífe.
[38] Fulfíll your prómise to your sérvant,
that yóu may be revéred.

[39] Túrn away the táunts I dréad,
for your decrées are góod.
[40] Sée, I lóng for your précepts;
give me lífe by your ríghteousness.

Psalm 119 (*118*)*:41–48*

Vau

[41] Lórd, let your lóve come upón me,
the salvátion you have prómised.
[42] I shall ánswer thóse who táunt me,
for I trúst in your wórd.

[43] Never táke the word of trúth from my móuth,
for I hópe in your decrées.
[44] I shall álways kéep your láw,
foréver and éver.

[45] I shall wálk on a spácious pláin,
for I séek your précepts.
[46] I will spéak of your decrées before rúlers,
and nót be abáshed.

[47] In your commánds I have fóund my delíght;
thése I have lóved.
[48] I reach óut to your commánds, which I lóve,
and pónder your státutes.

Psalm 119** (118)**:49–56
Zayin

[49] Remémber your wórd to your sérvant,
by which you máde me hópe.
[50] Thís is my cómfort in sórrow:
that your prómise gives me lífe.

[51] Though the próud may útterly derído me,
I do not túrn from your láw.
[52] When I remémber your júdgments of óld,
thése, O Lord, consóle me.

[53] I am séized with indignátion at the wícked
who forsáke your láw.
[54] Your státutes have becóme my sóng
wherévér I dwéll.

[55] I remémber your náme in the níghttime,
and I kéep your láw.
[56] Thís has béen my lót,
for I have képt your précepts.

Psalm 119 (*118*)*:57–64*
Heth

[57] Yóu, O Lórd, are my pórtion;
I have prómised to obéy your wórds.
[58] With all my héart I implóre your fávor;
as with your prómise, have mércy.

[59] Í have póndered my wáys,
and turned my stéps to your decrées.
[60] I make háste; I do nót deláy
to obéy your commánds.

[61] Though the néts of the wícked ensnáre me,
your láw I do nót forgét.
[62] At mídnight I will ríse and thánk you
for your ríghteous decrées.

[63] I am a fríend of áll who revére you,
who kéep your précepts.
[64] O Lord, your fáithful lóve fills the éarth.
Téach me your státutes.

Psalm 119** (118):**65–72
Teth

[65] O Lórd, you have been góod to your sérvant,
accórding to your wórd.
[66] Téach me good júdgment and knówledge,
for I trúst in your commánds.

[67] Befóre I was húmbled, I stráyed,
but nów I keep your wórd.
[68] You are góod, and you dó what is góod;
téach me your státutes.

[69] The árrogant sméar me with líes;
with all my héart I keep your précepts.
[70] Their héart is dénse like fát,
but your láw is my delíght.

[71] It was góod for mé to be húmbled,
that I might léarn your státutes.
[72] The láw from your móuth means móre to me
than large qúantities of sílver and góld.

Psalm 119 (118):73–80
Yod

[73] It was your hánds that máde me and sháped me;
grant me ínsight to léarn your commánds.
[74] Those who revére you sée me and rejóice,
for I trúst in your wórd.

[75] O Lord, I knów that your decrées are ríght,
and that in fáithfulness, you húmbled me.
[76] Let your fáithful lóve consóle me
by your prómise to your sérvant.

[77] Show me compássion, that Í may líve,
for your láw is my delíght.
[78] Let the árrogant be shámed who defléct me with
líes;
as for mé, I will pónder your précepts.

[79] Let those who féar you túrn to mé,
that they may knów your decrées.
[80] Let my héart be blámeless in your státutes,
that I may nót be put to sháme.

Psalm 119** (118):**81–88
Caph

[81] My soul yéarns for yóur salvátion;
I hópe in your wórd.
[82] My eyes yéarn to sée your prómise.
I ask, "Whén will you cómfort me?"

[83] I am like a wíneskin shríveled by smóke,
yet I remémber your státutes.
[84] How lóng must your sérvant endúre?
Whén will you bring júdgment on my fóes?

[85] For mé the próud have dug pítfalls;
they defý your láw.
[86] Your commánds are all trúe; then hélp me
when líes oppréss me.

[87] They have álmost made an énd of me on éarth,
yet I forsáke not your précepts.
[88] In your fáithful lóve, give me lífe;
I will obéy the decrées of your líps.

Psalm 119 *(118)****:89–96***
Lamed

[89] Forévér is your wórd, O Lórd,
standing fírm in the héavens.
[90] From áge to áge is your trúth;
like the éarth, it stands fírm.

[91] Your júdgments endúre to this dáy,
for áll things are your sérvants.
[92] Had your láw not béen my delíght,
I would have díed in my afflíction.

[93] I will néver forgét your précepts,
for with thém you give me lífe.
[94] Sáve me, Í am yóurs,
for I séek your précepts.

[95] Though the wícked lie in wáit to destróy me,
yet I pónder your decrées.
[96] I have séen that all perféction has an énd,
but your commánd is bóundless.

Psalm 119** (118)**:97–104
Mem

[97] O Lórd, how I lóve your láw:
my meditátion all the dáy!
[98] Your commánd makes me wíser than my fóes,
for it is wíth me álways.

[99] I have more ínsight than áll who téach me,
for I pónder your decrées.
[100] I have gáined more understánding than my
élders,
for I kéep your précepts.

[101] I keep my féet from évery evil páth,
to obéy your wórd.
[102] I have nót turned awáy from your decrées;
you yoursélf have táught me.

[103] How swéet is your prómise to my tóngue,
more than hóney in the móuth.
[104] I gáin understánding from your précepts,
and so I háte all false wáys.

Psalm 119** (118)**:105–112
Nun

[105] Your wórd is a lámp for my féet,
and a líght for my páth.
[106] I have swórn an óath and affírmed it,
to obéy your righteous júdgments.

[107] I am déeply afflícted, O Lórd;
by your wórd, give me lífe.
[108] Accépt, Lord, the hómage of my líps,
and téach me your decrées.

[109] My lífe is in my hánds at all tímes;
I do nót forget your láw.
[110] For me the wícked have sét a snáre;
yet I do not stráy from your précepts.

[111] Your decrées are my héritage foréver,
the jóy of my héart.
[112] I inclíne my heart to cárry out your státutes
foréver, to the énd.

Psalm 119 (118):113–120
Samech

[113] I have háted dóubtful thóughts,
but I lóve your láw.
[114] Yóu are my híding place, my shíeld;
I hópe in your wórd.

[115] Depárt from me, yóu who do évil;
I will kéep my God's commánds.
[116] Uphóld me by your prómise; I shall líve.
Let my hópes not be in váin.

[117] Bear me úp and Í shall be sáved,
and ever múse on your státutes.
[118] You spúrn all who stráy from your státutes;
their cúnning is in váin.

[119] You regárd the wícked like dróss,
so I lóve your decrées.
[120] My flesh trémbles in térror befóre you;
I féar your júdgments.

Psalm 119 *(118)*:***121–128***
Ayin

[121] I have dóne what is júst and ríghteous;
do not léave me to my fóes.
[122] Guarantée the well-béing of your sérvant;
let not the próud oppréss me.

[123] My eyes grow wéary as I wátch for your
salvátion,
and for your ríghteous prómise.
[124] Treat your sérvant with your fáithful lóve,
and téach me your státutes.

[125] I am your sérvant; gíve me understánding:
then I shall knów your decrées.
[126] It is tíme for the Lórd to áct,
for your láw has been bróken.

[127] That is whý I lóve your commánds
more than fínest góld,
[128] why I rúle my lífe by your précepts,
and háte false wáys.

Psalm 119 (118):129–136
Pe

[129] Your decrées are wónderful indéed;
therefore my sóul obéys them.
[130] The unfólding of your wórd gives líght,
and understánding to the símple.

[131] I have ópened my móuth and I sígh,
for I yéarn for your commánds.
[132] Túrn and have mércy on mé,
as is your rúle for those who lóve your náme.

[133] Let my stéps be guíded by your prómise;
may évil never rúle me.
[134] Redéem me from húman oppréssion,
and I will kéep your précepts.

[135] Let your fáce shine fórth on your sérvant,
and téach me your decrées.
[136] My éyes shed stréams of téars,
because of thóse who have not képt your láw.

Psalm 119 (118):137–144
Tsade

[137] Yóu are ríghteous, O LÓRD;
your júdgments are úpright.
[138] You have impósed your decrées with ríghteousness,
and with útter fidélity.

[139] Í am consúmed with zéal,
for my fóes forget your wórd.
[140] Your prómise has been thóroughly tésted,
and it is chérished by your sérvant.

[141] Although Í am yóung and despísed,
I do nót forget your précepts.
[142] Your ríghteousness is ríghteous foréver,
and your láw is trúth.

[143] Though ánguish and distréss have fóund me,
your commánds are my delíght.
[144] Your decrées are foréver júst;
give me ínsight, and Í shall líve.

Psalm 119 (118):145–152
Koph

[145] I cáll with all my héart; Lord, ánswer me.
I will obsérve your statutes.
[146] I cáll upón you; sáve me,
and I will kéep your decrées.

[147] I ríse before dáwn and cry for hélp;
I have hóped in your wórd.
[148] My éyes awáken before dáwn,
to pónder your prómise.

[149] In your mércy, héar my voice, O Lórd;
give me lífe by your decrées.
[150] Those who pursúe me with malíce draw néar;
they are fár from your láw.

[151] But yóu, O Lórd, are clóse;
all your commánds are trúth.
[152] From of óld I have knówn that your decrées
are estáblished forévér.

Psalm 119 *(118)***:153–160**
Resh

[153] Sée my afflíction and delíver me,
for I do nót forget your láw.
[154] Uphóld my cáuse and redéem me;
by your prómise, give me lífe.

[155] Salvátion is fár from the wícked,
who are héedless of your státutes.
[156] Númberless, Lórd, are your mércies;
in your jústice, give me lífe.

[157] Though my fóes and oppréssors are cóuntless,
I have not swérved from your decrées.
[158] I lóok at the fáithless with disgúst;
they have not képt your wórd.

[159] See how I lóve your précepts, O Lórd!
In your mércy, give me lífe.
[160] Trúth is the súm of your wórd;
all your righteous júdgments are etérnal.

Psalm 119 (118):161–168
Shin

[161] Though prínces oppréss me without cáuse,
my heart revéres your wórd.
[162] Í rejóice at your prómise,
like one who fínds a great tréasure.

[163] Fálsehood I háte and detést,
but I lóve your láw.
[164] Séven times a dáy I práise you
for your ríghteous decrées.

[165] The lóvers of your láw have great péace;
no stúmbling block for thém.
[166] I awáit your salvátion, O Lórd;
I fulfíll your commánds.

[167] My sóul obéys your decrées,
and lóves them déarly.
[168] I obéy your précepts and decrées;
all my wáys are befóre you.

Psalm 119 *(118)****:169–176***
Tau

[169] Let my crý come befóre you, O Lórd;
give me ínsight by your wórd.
[170] Let my pléading cóme befóre you;
rescue me accórding to your prómise.

[171] My líps shall procláim your práise,
because you téach me your státutes.
[172] My tóngue will síng of your prómise,
for your commánds are ríghteous.

[173] Let your hánd be réady to hélp me,
for I have chósen your précepts.
[174] I lóng for your salvátion, O Lórd,
and your láw is my delíght.

[175] My sóul shall líve and práise you.
Your júdgments give me hélp.
[176] I have stráyed like a shéep; seek your sérvant;
for I dó not forgét your commánds.

Psalm 120 *(119)*

[1] *A Song of Ascents.*

To the Lórd in the hóur of my distréss
I cáll—and am ánswered.
[2] "O Lórd, save my sóul from lying líps,
from the tóngue of the decéitful."

[3] Whát should God gíve you, what repáy you,
O decéitful tóngue?
[4] The wárrior's árrows shárpened,
with red-hot cóals from the bróom tree!

[5] Alás, that I sójourn in Méshech,
dwell amóng the tents of Kédar!
[6] Í have had enóugh of dwélling
with thóse who hate péace.
[7] Í am for péace, but when I spéak,
théy are for wár.

Psalm 121 *(120)*

[1] *A Song of Ascents.*

I líft up my éyes to the móuntains;
from whére shall come my hélp?
[2] My hélp shall cóme from the Lórd,
who made héaven and éarth.

[3] The Lord will kéep your fóot from stúmbling.
Your guárd will never slúmber.
[4] Nó, the guárdian of Ísrael
neither sléeps nor slúmbers.

[5] The Lord your guárd, the Lórd your sháde
at yóur right hánd.
[6] By dáy the sún shall not smíte you,
nor the móon in the níght.

[7] The Lórd will guárd you from évil,
will guárd your sóul.
[8] The Lord will guárd your góing and cóming,
both nów and forév er.

Psalm 122 (121)

[1] *A Song of Ascents. Of David.*

I rejóiced when they sáid to mé,
"Let us gó to the hóuse of the Lórd."
[2] And nów our féet are stánding
withín your gátes, O Jerúsalem.

[3] Jerúsalem is buílt as a cíty
bonded as óne togéther.
[4] It is thére that the tríbes go úp,
the tríbes of the Lórd,
as is decréed for Ísrael
to give thánks to the náme of the Lórd.

[5] Thére were set the thrónes for júdgment,
the thrónes of the hóuse of Dávid.
[6] For the péace of Jerúsalem práy,
"May they prósper, thóse who lóve you."
[7] May péace abíde in your wálls,
and secúrity bé in your tówers.

[8] For the sáke of my fámily and fríends,
let me sáy, "Péace upon yóu."
[9] For the sáke of the hóuse of the Lórd, our Gód,
I will séek good thíngs for yóu.

Psalm 123 (122)

[1] *A Song of Ascents.*

To yóu have I lífted up my éyes,
you who dwéll in the héavens.

[2] Behóld, like the éyes of sláves
on the hánd of their lórds,
líke the éyes of a sérvant
on the hánd of her místress,
so our éyes are on the Lórd our Gód,
till mércy be shówn us.

[3] Have mércy on us, Lórd, have mércy.
We are fílled with contémpt.
[4] Indéed, all too fúll is our sóul
with the scórn of the árrogant,
the disdáin of the próud.

Psalm 124 (123)

[1] *A Song of Ascents. Of David.*

"If the Lórd had not béen on our síde,"
let Ísrael sáy –
[2] "If the Lórd had not béen on our síde
when péople rose agáinst us,
[3] thén would they have swállowed us alíve
when their ánger was kíndled.

[4] "Thén would the wáters have engúlfed us,
the tórrent gone óver us;
[5] óver our héad would have swépt
the ráging wáters."

[6] Blést be the Lórd who did not gíve us
as préy to their téeth!
[7] Our lífe, like a bírd, has escáped
from the snáre of the fówler.

Indéed, the snáre has been bróken,
and wé have escáped.
[8] Our hélp is in the náme of the Lórd,
who made héaven and éarth.

Psalm 125 *(124)*

[1] *A Song of Ascents.*

Thóse who put their trúst in the Lórd
are like Mount Zíon, that cánnot be sháken,
that stánds foréver.
[2] Jerúsalem! The móuntains surróund her;
so the Lórd surróunds this péople,
both nów and foréver.

[3] For the scépter of the wícked shall not rést
over the lánd of the ríghteous,
for féar that the hánds of the ríghteous
should túrn to évil.

[4] Do góod, Lord, to thóse who are góod,
to the úpright of héart;
[5] but thóse who túrn to crooked wáys
the Lórd will drive awáy with the wícked!
On Ísrael, péace!

Psalm 126 *(125)*

[1] *A Song of Ascents.*

When the LÓRD brought back the éxiles of Zíon,
we thóught we were dréaming.
[2] Thén was our móuth filled with láughter;
on our tóngues, songs of jóy.

Thén they sáid among the nátions,
"What great déeds the LÓRD worked for thém!"
[3] What great déeds the LÓRD worked for ús!
Indéed, we were glád.

[4] Bring báck our éxiles, O LÓRD,
as stréams in the Négeb.
[5] Thóse who are sówing in téars
will síng when they réap.

[6] They go óut, they go óut, full of téars,
bearing séed for the sówing;
they come báck, they come báck with a sóng,
béaring their shéaves.

Psalm 127 (126)

[1] *A Song of Ascents. Of Solomon.*

If the Lórd does not buíld the hóuse,
in váin do its buílders lábor;
if the Lórd does not guárd the cíty,
in váin does the guárd keep wátch.

[2] In váin is your éarlier rísing,
your góing láter to rést,
you who tóil for the bréad you éat,
when God pours gífts on his belóved while they
slúmber.

[3] Yes, chíldren are a gíft from the Lórd,
a rewárd, the frúit of the wómb.
[4] Like árrows in the hánd of a wárrior,
so are the chíldren of one's yóuth.

[5] Bléssed áre the wárriors
who have fílled their quívers with these árrows!
They will háve no cáuse for sháme,
when they dispúte with their fóes in the gáteways.

Psalm 128 *(127)*

[1] *A Song of Ascents.*

Blessed are áll who féar the Lórd,
and wálk in God's wáys!
[2] By the lábor of your hánds you shall éat.
You will be bléssed and prósper.

[3] Your wífe is like a frúitful víne
in the héart of your hóuse;
your chíldren like shóots of the ólive
aróund your táble.
[4] Indéed thus sháll be bléssed
the húsband who féars the Lórd.

[5] Máy the Lord bléss you from Zíon.
May you sée Jerúsalem prósper
all the dáys of your lífe!
[6] May you sée your chíldren's chíldren.
On Ísrael, péace!

Psalm 129 (128)

[1] *A Song of Ascents.*

"They have préssed me hárd from my yóuth,"
let Ísrael síng.
[2] "They have préssed me hárd from my yóuth,
but could néver overcóme me.

[3] The plówers plówed my báck,
dráwing long fúrrows.
[4] Yét the LÓRD, who is ríghteous,
has cut the córds of the wícked."

[5] Lét them be shámed and róuted,
all thóse who hate Zíon!
[6] Lét them be like gráss on the róof
that wíthers befóre it flówers.

[7] With thát no réapers fíll their hánds,
no bínders of shéaves their árms.
[8] And thóse passing bý will not sáy,
"The bléssing of the LÓRD be upón you!"
We bléss you in the náme of the LÓRD!

Psalm 130 *(129)*

[1] *A Song of Ascents.*

Out of the dépths I crý to you, O Lórd;
[2] Lórd, hear my vóice!
O lét your éars be atténtive
to the sóund of my pléadings.

[3] If you, O Lórd, should márk iníquities,
Lórd, who could stánd?
[4] But with yóu is fóund forgíveness,
that yóu may be revéred.

[5] I wáit for the Lórd, my soul wáits.
I hópe in God's wórd.
[6] My sóul is wáiting for the Lórd,
móre than séntinels for dáybreak.

Móre than séntinels for dáybreak,
[7] let Ísrael wáit for the Lórd.
For with the Lórd there is lóving mércy,
in Gód is pléntiful redémption.
[8] It is the Lórd who will redéem Ísrael
from áll its iníquities.

Psalm 131 (130)

[1] *A Song of Ascents. Of David.*

O Lórd, my héart is not próud,
nor háughty my éyes.
I have not góne after thíngs too gréat,
nor márvels beyónd me.

[2] Trúly, I have sét my sóul
in tranquílity and sílence.
As a wéaned chíld on its móther,
as a weaned chíld is my sóul withín me.

[3] O Ísrael, hópe in the Lórd,
both nów and foréver.

Psalm 132 (131)

[1] *A Song of Ascents.*

O LÓRD, remémber Dávid
and áll the hárdships he endúred,
[2] the óath he swóre to the LÓRD,
his vów to the Stróng One of Jácob.

[3] "I will not énter the hóuse where I dwéll,
nor gó to the béd where I rést;
[4] I will gíve no sléep to my éyes,
to my éyelids I will gíve no slúmber,
[5] till I fínd a pláce for the LÓRD,
a dwélling for the Stróng One of Jácob."

[6] We héard of ít at Éphrata;
we fóund it in the pláins of Yéarim.
[7] "Let us gó to the pláce of God's dwélling;
lét us bow dówn at God's fóotstool."

[8] Go úp, LORD, to the pláce of your rést,
yóu and the árk of your stréngth.
[9] Your príests shall be clóthed with ríghteousness;
your fáithful shall ríng out their jóy.
[10] For the sáke of Dávid your sérvant,
dó not rejéct your anóinted.

[11] The LÓRD swore an óath to Dávid;
God will nót go báck on his wórd:
"A són, the frúit of your bódy,
will I sét upón your thróne.

[12] If your sóns hold fást to my cóvenant,
and my decrées that Í shall téach them,
their sóns, in túrn, shall sít
on your thróne from áge to áge."

[13] For the LÓRD has chósen Zíon,
has desíred it for a dwélling:
[14] "This is my résting place from áge to áge;
hére have I desíred to dwéll.

[15] "I will gréatly bléss her próduce;
I will fíll her póor with bréad.
[16] I will clóthe her príests with salvátion,
and her fáithful shall ríng out their jóy.

[17] "I will máke a stock spróut up for Dávid;
I will prepáre a lámp for my anóinted.
[18] I will cóver his énemies with sháme,
but on hím my crówn shall shíne."

Psalm 133 *(132)*

[1] *A Song of Ascents. Of David.*

How góod and how pléasant it ís,
when a fámily líves in únity!

[2] It is like précious óil upon the héad
running dówn upon the béard,
running dówn upon Áaron's béard,
upon the cóllar of his róbes;

[3] Like the déw of Hérmon, which runs dówn
on the móuntains of Zíon.
For thére the Lórd bestows a bléssing:
lífe forévěr.

Psalm 134 *(133)*

[1] *A Song of Ascents.*

O cóme and bléss the Lórd,
áll you sérvants of the Lórd,
who stand by níght in the hóuse of the Lórd.
[2] Lift up your hánds to the hóly pláce,
and bléss the Lórd.

[3] May the Lórd bléss you from Zíon,
who máde both héaven and éarth.

Psalm 135 (*134*)

1 Alleluia!

Práise the náme of the LÓRD;
give práise, O sérvants of the LÓRD,
2 who stánd in the hóuse of the LÓRD,
in the cóurts of the hóuse of our Gód.

3 Praise the LÓRD, for the LÓRD is góod.
Sing a psálm to God's náme, who is grácious.
4 For the LÓRD has chósen Jácob,
and Ísrael as a tréasured posséssion.

5 For I knów that the LÓRD is gréat,
that our Lórd is hígh above all góds.
6 Whatéver the LORD wílls is accómplished,
in héaven, ánd on éarth,
in the séas, and in áll the dépths.

7 God summons clóuds from the énds of the éarth,
makes líghtning prodúce the ráin,
sénds forth the wínd from heaven's tréasuries.

8 The Lord smóte the firstbórn of the Egýptians,
human béings and béasts alíke.
9 God sent sígns and wónders in your mídst, O
Égypt,
against Pháraoh and áll his sérvants.
10 Nátions in great númbers were strúck,
and kíngs in their míght were subdúed:

[11] Síhon, kíng of the Ámorites,
Óg, the kíng of Báshan,
and áll the kíngdoms of Cánaan.
[12] God gáve their lánd as a héritage,
a héritage to Ísrael, God's péople.

[13] LÓRD, your náme stands foréver,
your renówn, LORD, from áge to áge.
[14] For the LÓRD will víndicate this péople
and take píty on God's sérvants.

[15] Pagan ídols are sílver and góld,
the wórk of húman hánds.
[16] They have móuths but they dó not spéak;
they have éyes but they dó not sée.

[17] They have éars but they dó not héar;
there is néver a bréath on their líps.
[18] Their mákers will cóme to be like thém,
and só will áll who trúst in them!

[19] House of Ísrael, bléss the LÓRD!
House of Áaron, bléss the LÓRD!
[20] House of Lévi, bléss the LÓRD!
You who féar the LORD, bléss the LÓRD!
[21] From Zíon may the LÓRD be blést,
Gód, who dwélls in Jerúsalem!

Alleluia!

Psalm 136 (135)

[1] O give thánks to the LÓRD, who is góod,
for God's fáithful lóve endures foréver.
[2] Give thánks to the Gód of góds,
for God's fáithful lóve endures foréver.
[3] Give thánks to the Lórd of lórds,
for God's fáithful lóve endures foréver.

[4] Who alóne has wrought márvelous wórks,
for God's fáithful lóve endures foréver.
[5] who in wísdom máde the héavens,
for God's fáithful lóve endures foréver;
[6] who spréad the éarth on the wáters,
for God's fáithful lóve endures foréver.

[7] It was the Lórd who máde the great líghts,
for God's fáithful lóve endures foréver;
[8] the sún to rúle in the dáy,
for God's fáithful lóve endures foréver;
[9] the móon and the stárs in the níght,
for God's fáithful lóve endures foréver.

[10] The firstbórn of the Egýptians the Lord smóte,
for God's fáithful lóve endures foréver;
[11] brought Ísrael óut from their mídst,
for God's fáithful lóve endures foréver;
[12] with mighty hánd and óutstretched árm,
for God's fáithful lóve endures foréver.

[13] The Lord divíded the Réd Sea in twó,
for God's fáithful lóve endures forever;
[14] made Ísrael páss through the mídst,
for God's fáithful lóve endures forever;
[15] flung Pháraoh and his fórce in the Réd Sea,
for God's fáithful lóve endures forever.

[16] The Lord léd the péople through the désert,
for God's fáithful lóve endures forever.
[17] Kíngs in their gréatness he struck dówn,
for God's fáithful lóve endures forever.
[18] Kíngs in their spléndor the Lord sléw,
for God's fáithful lóve endures forever.

[19] Síhon, kíng of the Ámorites,
for God's fáithful lóve endures forever;
[20] and Óg, the kíng of Báshan,
for God's fáithful lóve endures forever.

[21] The Lord gáve their lánd as a héritage,
for God's fáithful lóve endures forever;
[22] A héritage for Ísrael, God's sérvant,
for God's fáithful lóve endures forever.
[23] The Lord remémbered us in óur distréss,
for God's fáithful lóve endures forever.

[24] The Lord snátched us awáy from our fóes,
for God's fáithful lóve endures forever.
[25] The Lord gives breád to all mórtal flésh,
for God's fáithful lóve endures forever.
[26] To the Gód of héaven give thánks,
for God's fáithful lóve endures forever.

Psalm 137 (136)

[1] By the rívers of Bábylon
thére we sat and wépt,
remémbering Zíon;
[2] on the póplars that gréw there
we húng up our hárps.

[3] For it was thére that they ásked us,
our cáptors, for sóngs,
our oppréssors, for jóy.
"Síng to us," they sáid,
"one of Zíon's sóngs."

[4] O hów could we síng
the sóng of the Lórd
on fóreign sóil?
[5] If I forgét you, Jerúsalem,
let my ríght hand wíther!

[6] O let my tóngue hold fást to my pálate
if I remémber you nót,
if I príze not Jerúsalem, the fírst of my jóys!

[7] Remémber, O Lórd,
against the chíldren of Édom
the dáy of Jerúsalem,
when they sáid, "Tear it dówn!
Tear it dówn to its foundátions!"

[8] O dáughter Bábylon, destróyer,
blessed who repáys you the páyment you páid to
  ús!
[9] Blessed who grásps and shátters your chíldren on
  the róck!

Psalm 138 (137)

[1] *Of David.*

I thánk you, Lórd, with all my héart;
you have héard the wórds of my móuth.
In the présence of the ángels I práise you.
[2] I bow dówn toward your hóly témple.

Í give thánks to your náme
for yóu have exálted over áll
your náme and your prómise.
[3] On the dáy I cálled, you ánswered me;
you incréased the stréngth of my sóul.

[4] All earthly rúlers shall thánk you, O Lórd,
when they héar the wórds of your móuth.
[5] They shall síng of the wáys of the Lórd,
"How gréat is the glóry of the Lórd!"

[6] The Lord is hígh, yet lóoks on the lówly,
and the háughty God knóws from afár.
[7] You give me lífe though I wálk amid afflíction;
you strétch out your hánd against the ánger of my
fóes.

With yóur right hánd you sáve me;
[8] the Lórd will accómplish this for mé.
O Lord, your mérciful lóve is etérnal;
discárd not the wórk of your hánds.

Psalm 139 (138)

[1] *For the Choirmaster. Of David. A Psalm.*

O Lórd, you séarch me and you knów me.
[2] You yoursélf know my résting and my rísing;
you discérn my thóughts from afár.
[3] You márk when I wálk or lie dówn;
you knów all my wáys through and thróugh.

[4] Before éver a wórd is on my tóngue,
you knów it, O Lórd, through and thróugh.
[5] Behínd and befóre, you besíege me,
your hánd ever láid upón me.
[6] Too wónderful for mé, this knówledge;
too hígh, beyónd my réach.

[7] O whére can I gó from your spírit,
or whére can I flée from your fáce?
[8] If I clímb the héavens, you are thére.
If I líe in Shéol, you are thére.

[9] If I táke the wíngs of the dáwn
or dwéll at the séa's furthest énd,
[10] even thére your hánd would léad me;
your right hánd would hóld me fást.

[11] If I sáy, “Let the dárkness híde me
and the líght aróund me be níght,”
[12] even dárkness is not dárk to yóu,
but níght will be bríght as the dáy,
and dárkness the sáme as the líght.

[13] For it was yóu who fórmed my inmost béing,
knit me togéther in my móther’s wómb.
[14] I thánk you who wónderfully máde me;
how wónderful áre your wórks,
which my sóul knows wéll!

[15] My fráme was not hídden from yóu,
when Í was being fáshioned in sécret
and mólded in the dépths of the éarth.

[16] Your éyes saw me yét unfórmed;
and all dáys are recórded in your bóok,
formed before óne of them cáme into béing.

[17] To me how précious your thóughts, O Gód;
how gréat is the súm of thém!
[18] If I cóunt them, they are móre than the sánd;
at the énd I am stíll at your síde.

[19] O Gód, that you would sláy the wícked;
let the blóodthirsty depárt from mé!
[20] With decéit they spéak against yóu,
and against yóu, they exált themselves in váin.

[21] Do Í not hate thóse who hate yóu,
abhor thóse who ríse against yóu?
[22] I háte them with a pérfect háte,
and théy are fóes to mé.

[23] O séarch me, Gód, and know my héart.
O tést me, and knów my thóughts.
[24] Sée that my páth is not wícked,
and léad me in the wáy everlásting.

Psalm 140 (*139*)

1 *For the Choirmaster. A Psalm of David.*

2 Réscue me, Lórd, from the wícked;
from the víolent kéep me sáfe,
3 from thóse who plan évil in their héarts,
and stír up strífe every dáy,
4 who shárpen their tóngue like an ádder's,
with the póison of víper on their líps.

5 Lord, guárd me from the hánds of the wícked;
from the víolent kéep me sáfe;
they plán to máke me stúmble.
6 The próud have hídden a tráp,
have spréad out línes in a nét,
set snáres acróss my páth.

7 I have sáid to the Lórd, "You are my Gód."
Give ear, O Lórd, to the crý of my appéal!
8 Lord, my Lórd, my míghty hélp,
you shíeld my héad in the báttle.
9 Do not gránt, O Lord, the wícked their desíre,
nor lét their plóts succéed.

[10] Those surróunding me líft up their héads.
Let the málice of their spéech overwhélm them.
[11] Let cóals of fíre rain upón them.
Let them be flúng in the abýss, no more to ríse.
[12] Let no slánderer stand fírm upon the éarth.
Let evil tráp the víolent to their rúin!

[13] I know the Lórd will avénge the póor,
that Gód will do jústice for the néedy.
[14] Truly the ríghteous will give thánks to your
náme;
the úpright shall líve in your présence.

Psalm 141 (140)

[1] *A Psalm of David.*

I have cálled to you, Lórd; O hásten to hélp me!
Héar my vóice when I crý to yóu.
[2] Lét my práyer be as íncense befóre you,
the ráising of my hánds like an évening oblátion.

[3] Sét, O Lórd, a guárd on my móuth;
keep wátch at the dóor of my líps!
[4] Do not túrn my héart to thíngs that are évil,
to wícked déeds with thóse who are sínners.

Néver allów me to sháre in their féasting.
[5] If sómeone ríghteous stríkes me it is kíndness;
but let the óil of the wícked not anóint my héad.
Let my práyer be éver agáinst their málice.

[6] If they fáll into the mérciless hánds of their júdges,
théy will grásp how kínd are my wórds.
[7] As clóds of éarth plowed úp on the gróund,
so their bónes were stréwn at the móuth of Shéol.

[8] To you my éyes are túrned, O Lórd, my Lórd.
In yóu I take réfuge; spáre my sóul!
[9] From the tráp they have láid for me, kéep me sáfe;
kéep me from the snáres of thóse who do évil.

[10] Let the wícked togéther fáll into their tráps,
while Í pursúe my wáy unhármed.

Psalm 142 *(141)*

[1] *A* Maskil *of David when he was in the cave.*
A Prayer.

[2] With my vóice I crý to you, O Lórd;
with my vóice I entréat you, O Lórd.
[3] I póur out my tróuble befóre you;
I recóunt to you áll my distréss
[4] while my spírit fáints withín me.
But yóu, O Lórd, know my páth.

On the wáy where Í shall wálk,
they have hídden a snáre to entráp me.
[5] Lóok on my right hánd and sée:
there is nó one who páys me héed.
No escápe remains ópen to mé;
nó one cáres for my sóul.

[6] To yóu I crý, O Lórd.
Í have said, "Yóu are my réfuge,
my pórtion in the lánd of the líving."
[7] Lísten, thén, to my crý,
for Í am brought dówn very lów.

Réscue me from thóse who pursúe me,
for théy are strónger than Í.
[8] Bríng my sóul out of príson,
and Í shall give thánks to your náme.
Aróund me the ríghteous will assémble,
becáuse of your góodness to mé.

Psalm 143 *(142)*

[1] *A Psalm of David.*

Lísten, O Lórd, to my práyer;
túrn your éar to my appéal.
You are fáithful, you are ríghteous; give ánswer.
[2] Do not cáll your sérvant to júdgment,
for in your síght no living béing is ríghteous.

[3] The fóe has pursúed my sóul,
has crúshed my lífe to the gróund,
and has máde me dwéll in dárkness,
like thóse long déad.
[4] Thérefore my spírit fáils;
my héart is désolate withín me.

[5] I remémber the dáys that are pást;
I pónder áll your wórks.
I múse on what your hánd has wróught,
[6] and to yóu I strétch out my hánds.
My sóul is like a párched land befóre you.

[7] O Lórd, make háste and ánswer me,
for my spírit fáils withín me.
Do not híde your fáce from mé,
lest I becóme like thóse going dówn to the pít.

[8] In the mórning, let me héar your faithful lóve,
for in yóu I pláce my trúst.
Make me knów the wáy I should wálk;
to yóu I líft up my sóul.

[9] Réscue me, O Lórd, from my fóes;
to yóu have I fléd for réfuge.
[10] Téach me to dó your wíll,
for yóu are my Gód.
Lét your good spírit guíde me
upon gróund that is lével.

[11] Lord, sáve my lífe for the sáke of your náme;
in your ríghteousness, léad my sóul out of
distréss.
[12] In your mércy make an énd of my fóes;
destroy all thóse who oppréss my sóul,
for Í am your sérvant.

Psalm 144 (143)

[1] *Of David.*

Blést be the Lórd, my róck,
who tráins my hánds for báttle,
my fíngers for wár.

[2] Gód is my lóve, my fórtress,
my strónghold, my sávior,
my shíeld in whóm I take réfuge,
who subdúes the péoples únder me.

[3] Lórd, who are wé that you regárd us so,
mere human béings, that you kéep us in mínd,
[4] péople who are mérely a bréath,
whose dáys are like a pássing shádow?

[5] Lower your héavens, O Lórd, and come dówn.
Touch the móuntains; wréathe them in smóke.
[6] Flash your líghtnings; róut the fóe.
Shoot your árrows, and pút them to flíght.

[7] Reach dówn with your hánd from on hígh;
rescue me, sáve me from the mány wáters,
from the hánds of fóreign fóes
[8] whose móuths speak émpty wórds,
whose hánds are ráised in pérjury.

[9] To you, O Gód, will I síng a new sóng;
I will pláy on the tén-stringed hárp
[10] to yóu who give kíngs their víctory,
who redéemed your sérvant Dávid,
from the évil swórd.

[11] Rescue me, frée me from the hánds of foreign
fóes,
whose móuths speak líes,
whose right hánds are ráised in pérjury.

[12] Let our sóns then flóurish like sáplings,
grown táll and stróng from their yóuth;
our dáughters gráceful as cólumns,
as thóugh they were cárved for a pálace.

[13] Let our bárns be filled to overflówing
with cróps of évery kínd;
our shéep incréasing by thóusands,
téns of thóusands in our fíelds,
[14] our cáttle héavy with yóung.

No rúined wáll, no éxile,
no sóund of wéeping in our stréets.
[15] Blessed the péople of whóm this is trúe;
blessed the péople whose Gód is the Lórd!

Psalm 145 (144)

[1] *Praise. Of David.*

I will extól you, my Gód and Kíng,
and bless your náme foréver and éver.

[2] I will bléss you dáy after dáy,
and praise your náme foréver and éver.
[3] The LORD is gréat and híghly to be práised;
God's gréatness cánnot be méasured.

[4] Age to áge shall procláim your wórks,
shall decláre your míghty déeds.
[5] They will téll of your great glóry and spléndor,
and recóunt your wónderful wórks.

[6] They will spéak of your áwesome déeds,
recóunt your gréatness and míght.
[7] They will recáll your abúndant góodness,
and síng of your ríghteous deeds with jóy.

[8] The LORD is kínd and fúll of compássion,
slow to ánger, abóunding in mércy.
[9] How góod are you, O LÓRD, to áll,
compássionate to áll your créatures.

[10] All your wórks shall thánk you, O LÓRD,
and áll your fáithful ones bléss you.
[11] They shall spéak of the glóry of your réign,
and decláre your míghty déeds,

[12] To make knówn your míght to the whóle human
ráce,
and the glórious spléndor of your réign.
[13] Your kíngdom is an éverlasting kíngdom;
your rule endúres for áll generátions.

You are fáithful, LÓRD, in all your wórds,
and hóly in áll your déeds.
[14] Yóu, LORD, suppórt all who fáll,
and ráise up áll who are bowed dówn.

[15] The éyes of áll look to yóu,
and you gíve them their fóod in due séason.
[16] You ópen your hánd and sátisfy
the desíre of every líving thíng.

[17] You are ríghteous, O LÓRD, in all your wáys,
and hóly in áll your déeds.
[18] You are clóse, LORD, to áll who cáll on you,
who cáll on yóu in trúth.

[19] You fulfíll the desíres of those who féar you;
you héar their crý and sáve them.
[20] You keep wátch, LORD, over áll who lóve you;
but the wícked you will útterly destróy.

[21] Let my móuth speak the práise of the LÓRD;
let all flésh bless the hóly náme
forever, for áges unénding.

Psalm 146 *(145)*

[1] Alleluia!

My sóul, give práise to the LÓRD;
[2] I will práise the LÓRD all my lífe,
sing práise to my Gód while I líve.

[3] Pút no trúst in rúlers,
in human béings who cánnot sáve.
[4] Take their bréath, they retúrn to the éarth,
and their pláns that dáy come to nóthing.

[5] Blessed the óne who is hélped by Jacob's Gód,
whose hópe is in the LÓRD our Gód,
[6] who máde the héavens and the éarth,
the séas and áll they contáin,

Who presérves fidélity forév er,
[7] who does jústice to thóse who are oppréssed.
who fúrnishes bréad to the húngry;
the LÓRD who sets prísoners frée,
[8] the LORD who ópens the éyes of the blínd,
the LORD who ráises up thóse who are bowed
dówn.

It is the Lórd who lóves the ríghteous,
[9] the Lórd who protécts the stránger
and uphólds the órphan and the wídow,
but thwárts the páth of the wícked.
[10] The Lórd will réign foréver,
your God, O Zíon, from áge to áge.

Alleluia!

Psalm 147A *(146:1–11)*

Alleluia!

[1] How góod to sing psálms to our Gód;
how pléasant to chant fítting práise!

[2] The Lórd builds úp Jerúsalem
and bríngs back Ísrael's éxiles;
[3] God héals the brókenhéarted,
and bínds up áll their wóunds;
[4] God cóunts out the númber of the stárs,
and cálls each óne by its náme.

[5] Our Lórd is gréat and almíghty;
God's wísdom can néver be méasured.
[6] The Lórd lifts úp the lówly,
and casts dówn the wícked to the gróund.
[7] O síng to the Lórd, giving thánks;
sing psálms to our Gód with the lýre.

[8] The Lord cóvers the héavens with clóuds;
and prepáres the ráin for the éarth,
making móuntains sprόut with gráss,
and plánts to sérve human néeds.

[9] God provídes the cáttle with their fóod,
and whát young rávens cáll for.
[10] The Lord's delíght is nót in the stréngth of hórses,
nor God's pléasure in a wárrior's stríde.
[11] The Lord delíghts in thóse who revére him,
those who wáit for God's fáithful lóve.

Psalm 147B (*147*)

[12] O Jerúsalem, glórify the Lórd!
O Zíon, práise your Gód,
[13] who has stréngthened the bárs of your gátes,
and has blégssed your chíldren withín you;
[14] who estáblished péace on your bórders,
and gíves you your fíll of finest whéat.

[15] The Lord sénds out his wórd to the éarth;
the divíne commánd runs swíftly.
[16] God shówers down snów like wóol,
and scátters hóarfrost like áshes.

[17] The Lord húrls down háilstones like crúmbs;
befóre such cóld, who can stánd?
[18] God sénds forth a wórd and it mélts them;
at the blówing of God's bréath the waters flów.

[19] The Lord revéals a wórd to Jácob;
to Ísrael, decrées and júdgments.
[20] God has nót dealt thús with other nátions,
has not táught them héaven's júdgments.

Alleluia!

Psalm 148

[1] Alleluia!

Práise the LÓRD from the héavens;
práise the Lórd in the héights.
[2] Práise the Lord, áll his ángels;
práise the Lord, áll his hósts.

[3] Práise the Lord, sún and móon;
práise the Lord, all shíning stárs.
[4] Práise the Lórd, highest héavens,
and the wáters abóve the héavens.

[5] Let them práise the náme of the LÓRD,
who commánded, and théy were created.
[6] God estáblished them forever and éver,
gave a láw which shall nót pass awáy.

[7] Práise the LÓRD from the éarth,
sea créatures and all ócean dépths,
[8] fire and háil, snów and míst,
stormy wínds that fulfíll the commánd;

[9] Móuntains ánd all hílls,
frúit trees ánd all cédars,
[10] béasts, both wíld and táme,
créeping things and bírds on the wíng;

[11] Rúlers of the éarth and all péoples,
sóvereigns and all júdges of the éarth,
[12] young mén and máidens as wéll,
the óld and the yóung togéther.

[13] Let them práise the náme of the Lórd,
for God's náme alóne is exálted,
whose splendor ríses above héaven and éarth.

[14] The Lord exálts the stréngth of the péople,
and is the práise of áll the fáithful,
the práise of the chíldren of Ísrael,
of the péople to whóm our God is clóse.

Alleluia!

Psalm 149

[1] Alleluia!

Síng a new sóng to the Lórd,
high práise in the assémbly of the fáithful.
[2] Let Ísrael rejóice in its Máker;
let Zion's chíldren exúlt in their Kíng.
[3] Let them práise God's náme with dáncing,
and make músic with tímbrel and lýre.

[4] For the Lórd takes delíght in the péople,
and adórns the póor with salvátion.
[5] Let the fáithful rejóice in glóry,
shóut with jóy on their cóuches.
[6] Let the práise of Gód be in their móuths
and a twó-edged swórd in their hánds,

[7] To déal out véngeance to the nátions
and púnishment upón the péoples;
[8] to bínd their rúlers in cháins
and their nóbles in fétters of íron;
[9] to cárry out the júdgment decréed.
This is an hónor for áll God's fáithful.

Alleluia!

Psalm 150

[1] Alleluia!

Praise Gód in the hóly témple;
praise the Lórd in the míghty fírmament.
[2] Praise Gód for pówerful déeds;
for bóundless grándeur, praise Gód.

[3] O praise the Lórd with sóund of trúmpet;
give práise with lúte and hárp.
[4] Praise Gód with tímbrel and dánce;
give práise with stríngs and pípes.

[5] O praise Gód with resóunding cýmbals;
give práise with cláshing of cýmbals.
[6] Let éverything that bréathes praise the LÓRD!

Alleluia!

The following tones are available for purchase from GIA Publications, Inc.

Conception Abbey Tones Accompaniment G-7984K
Conception Abbey Tones Melody Card. G-7984A